Blend-It Books

Houghton Mifflin Harcourt

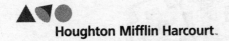

Houghton Mifflin Harcourt

What is the purpose of the Blend-It Books?

The **Blend-It Books** provide engaging, highly decodable texts (75% or more decodable words) for independent blending and reading practice, to promote decoding automaticity and fluency. For each sound-spelling reviewed or introduced in Grade 2 of the Houghton Mifflin Harcourt *Journeys* program, two four-page books feature the skill within connected text. For sounds with multiple spellings, two sound-spellings are sometimes paired in the same books for comparison. For example, there are two books for the short *o* sound. For the long *o* sound, there are two books for the *o_e* spelling, and two for the *oa* and *ow* spellings. Later in the year, two more books feature all those known spellings in longer words.

In addition, the **Blend-It Books** provide practice for key structural analysis skills. For example, for the *-ed* inflection there are two books for *each* pronunciation: /ĕd/, /d/, and /t/. Later in the year, four more books feature *-ed*, this time using words with spelling changes (dropped final *e*, doubled final consonant) before the inflection.

The text for each book also includes a smaller number (25% or fewer) of high-frequency words taught previously in *Journeys*. Those words were drawn from research studies on the most commonly used words in English, and words were chosen only when they received high scores on multiple lists.

For reference, the back of each book lists all the decodable words, decoding skills, and high-frequency words featured in that selection. A summary list inside the back cover shows all the decoding skills and high-frequency words taught to date in *Journeys*.

How are the Blend-It Books organized?

The **Blend-It Books** are numbered sequentially and reflect the order of the decoding skills taught in each unit of *Journeys*. The chart on the following pages lists all the books for Grade 2.
Volume 1: Books 1–92 for the skills in Units 1–2
Volume 2: Books 93–188 for the skills in Units 3–6

When do I use the Blend-It Books?

- Users of *Journeys* will find references to corresponding **Blend-It Books** in the phonics lessons in the Teacher's Editions.
- The books are also an excellent resource any time a child needs extra practice reading words with a specific sound/spelling.

How can I use the Blend-It Books to meet specific needs?

- Help children differentiate between two or more similar sound/spellings by reading and comparing books that feature them.
- Have English learners focus on sounds and spellings they find difficult in English by reading books chorally with an adult.
- Informally assess children's understanding of a new skill by having them read a book aloud to you.

What are the options for setting up the Blend-It Books?

- The books are available as blackline masters for copying, or in digital files that can be read onscreen or downloaded.
- Provide children with the books only as they need them, or set up the numbered books for children to access on their own all year.
- Make copies for children to read and color in class or take home, or prepare a laminated set for use at school.
- Set up a chart for children to track their own progress as they read.

Jill Is Sick

DECODABLE WORDS

Target Skill: short *i*

big	it	sits
hit	Jill	still
in	Jill's	will
is	sick	win

Previously Taught Skills

and	glad	on
bed	got	play
but	mom	rest
can	must	well
day	not	yay

SKILLS APPLIED IN WORDS IN STORY: short *a*; short *i*   **From Grade 1:** consonants; short vowels; double final consonants *ll*; consonants *-ck*; blends with *l*; blends with *s*; final blends: *nd*; final blends *st*; base words and ending *-s*; possessives with *'s*; long *a* (*ay*)

HIGH-FREQUENCY WORDS

a	have	she	today
are	her	soon	wants
comes	next	the	what
do	said	to	you

© Houghton Mifflin Harcourt Publishing Company

Houghton Mifflin Harcourt

Jill Is Sick

High-Frequency Words Taught to Date

Grade 1

a	bring	everyone	he	many	party	studied	was
about	brothers	eyes	head	maybe	people	sure	wash
above	brown	fall	hear	me	pictures	surprised	watch
across	buy	family	heard	minute	play	take	water
after	by	far	help	more	please	talk	we
again	call	father	her	most	pull	teacher	were
all	car	few	here	mother	pushed	the	what
almost	carry	field	high	my	put	their	where
along	caught	find	hold	myself	read	there	who
always	city	first	house	near	ready	these	why
and	cold	five	how	never	right	they	window
animal	come	fly	I	new	said	think	with
are	could	follow	idea	night	school	those	work
around	country	food	into	no	second	thought	world
away	covers	for	is	noise	see	three	would
baby	cried	four	kinds	nothing	seven	to	write
ball	different	friend	know	now	shall	today	years
be	do	friendship	large	of	she	together	yellow
bear	does	full	laugh	off	should	too	you
beautiful	done	funny	learning	old	show	took	young
because	don't	give	light	once	sing	toward	your
been	door	go	like	one	small	try	
before	down	goes	listen	only	soil	two	*Grade 2*
began	draw	good	little	open	some	under	next
begins	earth	great	live	or	sometimes	until	
bird	eat	green	long	our	soon	use	
blue	eight	ground	look	out	sorry	very	
both	enough	grow	loudly	over	starts	walk	
boy	even	happy	loved	own	stories	want	
	every	have	make	paper	story	warms	

Decoding skills taught to date: short *a,* short *i* **From Grade 1:** consonants; short vowels; double final consonants: *ll*; final blends: *nd*; consonants *-ck*; blends with *l*; blends with *s*; final blends *st*; base words and ending *-s*; possessives with *'s*; long *a (ay)*

Jill Is Sick

Jill will have a big day. Jill's big day is soon. Jill will play on the big day, but will she win?

1

The next day, Jill is glad. She is not sick! She can play!

It is Jill's big day.

Jill got a hit. Yay, Jill!

4

Jill sits in bed and is not well. Jill is sick.

But Jill still wants to play on her big day. What can Jill do?

Jill's mom comes in. She sits on Jill's bed.

"Jill, you are sick," said Jill's mom. "Today you must rest."

In the Hot Sand

DECODABLE WORDS

Target Skill: **short *i***

did	dip	in	Kim	will
dig	hit	is	Sid	
digs	hits	it	Tim	

Previously Taught Skills

and	fun	sand
but	get	stands
can	hot	

SKILLS APPLIED IN WORDS IN STORY: short *a*   **From Grade 1:** consonants;
short vowels; double final consonants: *ll*; blends with *s*; final blends: *nd*; base words and
ending *-s*

HIGH-FREQUENCY WORDS

a	he	take
ball	make	the
go	play	what

© Houghton Mifflin Harcourt Publishing Company

In the Hot Sand

Tick, Tock!

DECODABLE WORDS

Target Skill: **short o**

dog	mom	Rob	stop
got	moss	rock	tock
hot	on	Roz	Todd
lot	pond	shops	Todd's

Previously Taught Skills

and	I	it's	tick
did	in	lunch	went
has	is	Miss	with
hi	it	past	

SKILLS APPLIED IN WORDS IN STORY: short *a*; short *i*; short *o*   **From Grade 1:**
consonants; short vowels; double final consonants: *ss*; consonants: *ck*; blends with *s*;
final blends: *nt*, *nd*, *st*; digraphs: *th*, *ch*, *sh*; possessives with *'s*; contractions with *'s*;
long *i* (*i*); base words and ending *-s*

HIGH-FREQUENCY WORDS

a	said	there	to
car	school	they	today
for	the	time	

Tick, Tock!

Houghton Mifflin Harcourt.

High-Frequency Words Taught to Date

Grade 1

a	bring	everyone	he	many	party	studied	was
about	brothers	eyes	head	maybe	people	sure	wash
above	brown	fall	hear	me	pictures	surprised	watch
across	buy	family	heard	minute	play	take	water
after	by	far	help	more	please	talk	we
again	call	father	her	most	pull	teacher	were
all	car	few	here	mother	pushed	the	what
almost	carry	field	high	my	put	their	where
along	caught	find	hold	myself	read	there	who
always	city	first	house	near	ready	these	why
and	cold	five	how	never	right	they	window
animal	come	fly	I	new	said	think	with
are	could	follow	idea	night	school	those	work
around	country	food	into	no	second	thought	world
away	covers	for	is	noise	see	three	would
baby	cried	four	kinds	nothing	seven	to	write
ball	different	friend	know	now	shall	today	years
be	do	friendship	large	of	she	together	yellow
bear	does	full	laugh	off	should	too	you
beautiful	don't	funny	learning	old	show	took	young
because	done	give	light	once	sing	toward	your
been	door	go	like	one	small	try	
before	down	goes	listen	only	soil	two	**Grade 2**
began	draw	good	little	open	some	under	children
begins	earth	great	live	or	sometimes	until	next
bird	eat	green	long	our	soon	use	
blue	eight	ground	look	out	sorry	very	
both	enough	grow	loudly	over	starts	walk	
boy	even	happy	loved	own	stories	want	
	every	have	make	paper	story	warms	

Decoding skills taught to date: short *a;* short *i;* CVC syllable pattern; short *o* **From Grade 1:** consonants; short vowels; double final consonants: *ss;* consonants: *ck;* blends with *s;* final blends: *nt, nd, st;* digraphs: *th, ch, sh;* possessives with *'s;* contractions with *'s;* long *i (i);* base words and ending *-s*

Tick, tock! Tick, tock!

Todd did a lot today. There is Todd's mom.

"Hi, mom!"

Tick, Tock!

Tick, tock! Tick, tock!

Todd and Mom got in the car. They went past shops. They got to school.

"Stop," said Todd.

Tick, tock! Tick, tock!

It's time for lunch. Todd got a hot

dog. Rob got a lot!

Tick, tock! Tick, tock!

Todd went to the pond with Miss Roz.

"I got a rock," said Todd. "It has

moss on it."

Big Hot Pot

DECODABLE WORDS

Target Skill: **Short *o***

hot	not	pot
job	on	stop
lot	Pop	

Previously Taught Skills

am	gave	has	is	that
and	get	him	it	things
ask	getting	his	lid	this
big	glad	I	made	will
can	grins	in	takes	yum

SKILLS APPLIED IN WORDS IN STORY: short *a*; short *i*; short *o* **From Grade 1:** consonants; short vowels; inflection -*s*; blends with *l*; blends with *r*; final blends *nd*; digraph *th*; base words and endings -*s*, -*ing*; long *a* (*a_e*); long *i* (*i*); words ending with *ng*

HIGH-FREQUENCY WORDS

a	help	put	time
do	me	puts	to
he	my	the	

Houghton Mifflin Harcourt.

Big Hot Pot

What a Mess!

DECODABLE WORDS

Target Skill: Short *e*

bed	Fred	met	well
bet	help	next	went
Beth	left	red	yes
Beth's	let's	shed	yet
dress	mess	tell	

Previously Taught Skills

and	doll	lots	sock
asked	he	on	this
big	I	pick	too
can	in	room	toys
Dad	is	rug	up
did	it	see	you

SKILLS APPLIED IN WORDS IN STORY: short *a*; short *i*; CVC syllable pattern; short *o*; short *u*; short *e*   **From Grade 1:** consonants; short vowels; final double consonants *ll*; final double consonants *ss*; consonants *ck*; long *e* (CV, *ee*); long *i* (CV); inflections -*s*, -*ed*; blends with *r*; final blends; final blend *nt*; final blend *nd*; digraph *th*; possessives with *'s*; digraph *sh*; digraph *wh*; contractions with *'s*; vowel digraphs/spelling patterns *oo*, *ou*; vowel combination *oy*

HIGH-FREQUENCY WORDS

a	said	to	were
of	the	was	what

© Houghton Mifflin Harcourt Publishing Company

What a Mess!

High-Frequency Words Taught to Date

Grade 1

a	bring	everyone	he	many	party	studied	was
about	brothers	eyes	head	maybe	people	sure	wash
above	brown	fall	hear	me	pictures	surprised	watch
across	buy	family	heard	minute	play	take	water
after	by	far	help	more	please	talk	we
again	call	father	her	most	pull	teacher	were
all	car	few	here	mother	pushed	the	what
almost	carry	field	high	my	put	their	where
along	caught	find	hold	myself	read	there	who
always	city	first	house	near	ready	these	why
and	cold	five	how	never	right	they	window
animal	come	fly	I	new	said	think	with
are	could	follow	idea	night	school	those	work
around	country	food	into	no	second	thought	world
away	covers	for	is	noise	see	three	would
baby	cried	four	kinds	nothing	seven	to	write
ball	different	friend	know	now	shall	today	years
be	do	friendship	large	of	she	together	yellow
bear	does	full	laugh	off	should	too	you
beautiful	don't	funny	learning	old	show	took	young
because	done	give	light	once	sing	toward	your
been	door	go	like	one	small	try	
before	down	goes	listen	only	soil	two	**Grade 2**
began	draw	good	little	open	some	under	children
begins	earth	great	live	or	sometimes	until	next
bird	eat	green	long	our	soon	use	
blue	eight	ground	look	out	sorry	very	
both	enough	grow	loudly	over	starts	walk	
boy	even	happy	loved	own	stories	want	
	every	have	make	paper	story	warms	

Decoding skills taught to date: short *a;* short *i;* CVC syllable pattern; short *o;* short *u;* short *e* **From Grade 1:** consonants; short vowels; final double consonants *ll;* final double consonants *ss;* consonants *ck;* long *e* (CV, *ee*); long *i;* inflections *-s, -ed;* blends with *r;* final blends; final blend *nt;* final blend *nd;* digraph *th;* possessives with *'s;* digraph *sh;* digraph *wh;* contractions with *'s;* vowel digraphs/spelling patterns *oo, ou;* vowel combination *oy*

What a Mess!

"Let's tell Beth to pick up this mess," said Fred.

"Well, can Fred help?" Beth asked Dad.

"Yes, Fred can help!"

Dad went to Beth's room. A doll in a dress and a red sock were on Beth's bed. Lots of toys were on Beth's rug.

"What a mess!" said Dad.

4

1

Dad left Beth's mess. He met Fred in the next room.

"Did you see Beth yet?" asked Dad.

"I bet Beth is in the shed," said Fred.

Fred and Dad went to the shed. Beth was in the shed. It was a big mess, too!

"This is a mess!" said Dad.

Dogs at the Vet

DECODABLE WORDS

Target Skill: Short *e*

Ed	met	pets	them	wet
get	Peg	Ted	vet	yell
Jed	pet	tells	went	yet

Previously Taught Skills

and	go	it's	snacks
at	good	like	take
back	has	look	time
but	he	not	with
Dad	hide	out	
dogs	is	run	
for	it	sits	

SKILLS APPLIED IN WORDS IN STORY: short *a*; short *i*; CVC syllable pattern; short *o*; short *u*; short *e* **From Grade 1:** consonants; inflection -*s*; short vowels; double final consonants *ll*; consonants *ck*; blends with *s*; final blend *nt*; final blend *nd*; digraph *th*; *r*-controlled vowel *or*; long *a* (CVC*e*); long *e* (CV); long *i* (CVC*e*); long *o* (CV); vowel digraph /o͞o/ *oo*; *vowel combination ou*; contractions with '*s*

HIGH-FREQUENCY WORDS

are	do	the	to
children	have	they	want

▲◆● Houghton Mifflin Harcourt.

Dogs at the Vet

Mom made this frame. Kate plays a whale. Dave has a big mane. What is Dave?

© Houghton Mifflin Harcourt Publishing Company

Kate Has Frames

Kate takes pictures. This frame has her pals, Dave and Nate. Dave can run. Nate can run. Did Dave win? Did Nate win?

What is in this frame? Kate wades
with Dave in big waves. The waves are
big, big, big. A big wave hits Kate. A big
wave hits Dave. Kate has fun. Dave
has fun.

Dad made this frame. Kate waves to
Dad. Kate ate cake. The cake looks like
a plane.

Bake Sale

DECODABLE WORDS

Target Skill: **long _a_ (CVC_e_)**

bake	Dale	make	take
cake	Jake	Nate	
cakes	Lane	sale	

Previously Taught Skills

and	fun	nut	stop
at	get	sell	that
big	is	sick	this
can	mix	six	well
drops	Mom	stand	will

SKILLS APPLIED IN WORDS IN STORY: short _a_; short _e;_ short _i_; short _u_; short _o_; CVC syllable pattern (closed syllables); long _a_ (CVC_e_) **From Grade 1:** consonants; short vowels; consonants _ck_; final blend _nd_; inflection _-s_; _r_ blends; _s_ blends; double consonants _ll_; digraph _th_

HIGH-FREQUENCY WORDS

a	have	look	the	what
children	help	next	they	writes
give	I	said	to	

Houghton Mifflin Harcourt

Bake Sale

High-Frequency Words Taught to Date

Grade 1							
a	bring	everyone	he	many	party	studied	was
about	brothers	eyes	head	maybe	people	sure	wash
above	brown	fall	hear	me	pictures	surprised	watch
across	buy	family	heard	minute	play	take	water
after	by	far	help	more	please	talk	we
again	call	father	her	most	pull	teacher	were
all	car	few	here	mother	pushed	the	what
almost	carry	field	high	my	put	their	where
along	caught	find	hold	myself	read	there	who
always	city	first	house	near	ready	these	why
and	cold	five	how	never	right	they	window
animal	come	fly	I	new	said	think	with
are	could	follow	idea	night	school	those	work
around	country	food	into	no	second	thought	world
away	covers	for	is	noise	see	three	would
baby	cried	four	kinds	nothing	seven	to	write
ball	different	friend	know	now	shall	today	years
be	do	friendship	large	of	she	together	yellow
bear	does	full	laugh	off	should	too	you
beautiful	done	funny	learning	old	show	took	young
because	don't	give	light	once	sing	toward	your
been	door	go	like	one	small	try	
before	down	goes	listen	only	soil	two	Grade 2
began	draw	good	little	open	some	under	children
begins	earth	great	live	or	sometimes	until	next
bird	eat	green	long	our	soon	use	
blue	eight	ground	look	out	sorry	very	
both	enough	grow	loudly	over	starts	walk	
boy	even	happy	loved	own	stories	want	
	every	have	make	paper	story	warms	

Decoding skills taught to date: short *a*; short *i*; short *o*; short *u*; short *e*; CVC syllable pattern (closed syllables); long *a* (CVC*e*) **From Grade 1:** consonants; short vowels; consonants *ck*; final blend *nd*; inflection *-s*; *r* blends; *s* blends; double consonants *ll*; digraph *th*

Bake Sale

The bake sale is fun! Children stop at the bake sale.

"I will take that big cake!" said Nate.

"I will take six nut drops," said Lane.

Jake and Dale can bake. What will Jake and Dale bake? They will bake big cakes. Mom will help Jake and Dale bake cakes. Jake can mix and mix.

The corn is hot, hot, hot. It is time to eat it. Cal does not cut the corn. Cal likes to eat corn on the cob. Cal can bite the corn. Cal, Mom, and Dad like to eat the corn they just picked.

4

Cal Likes Corn

The corn is big and ripe. It is time to pick it. Mom and Dad have a lot of corn to pick and no time to pick it. Cal helps Mom and Dad pick the corn. Cal, Mom, and Dad make a good team! Cal has fun when she helps Mom and Dad.

1

It is time to clean the corn. Cal cleans the corn she picked. She rubs it and wipes it with a napkin. Mom cuts the corn for Cal. Cal wipes and Mom cuts. Cal and Mom make a good team!

Mom has a big pot. Cal puts one corn in at a time. Next, the big pot gets hot. Mom helps Cal with the hot pot. Cal wants the corn to get hot fast.

Cal and Cam

DECODABLE WORDS

Target Skill: /k/ Spelled *c*

Cal	can	caps
Cam	cap	cop

Previously Taught Skills

a	five	like	play	which
and	fun	makes	sad	will
as	has	mom	tells	yells
asks	his	not	ten	yes
at	I	pal	time	
best	is	pals	wait	
but	it	plan	well	

SKILLS APPLIED IN WORDS IN STORY: short *a*; short *i*; short *o*; short *u*; short *e*; long *a* (CVCe); long *i* (CVCe); /k/ spelled *c* **From Grade 1:** consonants; short vowels; initial and final blends; inflection *-s*; /z/ spelled *s*; long *a* spelled *ay*, *ai*; double final consonants; long *i* spelled *i*; digraphs

HIGH-FREQUENCY WORDS

a	do	house	then	you
all	does	now	they	
are	go	over	to	
call	have	see	want	
come	he	the	with	

© Houghton Mifflin Harcourt Publishing Company

Cal and Cam

High-Frequency Words Taught to Date

Grade 1

a	brown	far	here	myself	right	those	would
about	buy	father	high	near	said	thought	write
above	by	few	hold	never	school	three	years
across	call	field	house	new	second	to	yellow
after	car	find	how	night	see	today	you
again	carry	first	I	no	seven	together	young
all	caught	five	idea	noise	shall	too	your
almost	city	fly	into	nothing	she	took	
along	cold	follow	is	now	should	toward	**Grade 2**
always	come	food	kinds	of	show	try	children
and	could	for	know	off	sing	two	next
animal	country	four	large	old	small	under	other
are	covers	friend	laugh	once	soil	until	this
around	cried	friendship	learning	one	some	use	
away	different	full	light	only	sometimes	very	
baby	do	funny	like	open	soon	walk	
ball	does	give	listen	or	sorry	want	
be	done	go	little	our	starts	warms	
bear	don't	goes	live	out	stories	was	
beautiful	door	good	long	over	story	wash	
because	down	great	look	own	studied	watch	
been	draw	green	loudly	paper	sure	water	
before	earth	ground	loved	party	surprised	we	
began	eat	grow	make	people	take	were	
begins	eight	happy	many	pictures	talk	what	
bird	enough	have	maybe	play	teacher	where	
blue	even	he	me	please	the	who	
both	every	head	minute	pull	their	why	
boy	everyone	hear	more	pushed	there	window	
bring	eyes	heard	most	put	these	with	
brothers	fall	help	mother	read	they	work	
	family	her	my	ready	think	world	

Decoding skills taught to date: short *a*; short *i*; short *o*; short *u*; short *e*; closed syllables; long *a* (CVC*e*); long *i* (CVC*e*); /k/ spelled *c* **From Grade 1:** consonants; short vowels; initial and final blends; inflection *-s*; /z/ spelled *s*; long *a* spelled *ay*, *ai*; double final consonants; long *i* spelled *i*; digraphs

It is five and Cal has to go. Cam does not want Cal to go but he is not sad. Cam and Cal have a plan! Cam will go with Cal and his mom. They will play at his house now. Cam and Cal are best pals!

4

Cal and Cam

Cam makes a call to his best pal Cal. "Cal, can you play at ten?" asks Cam.

"Yes!" Cal tells Cam. "I will go over then."

"See you at ten," Cam tells Cal. "I can not wait!"

1

Cole Woke Up

DECODABLE WORDS

Target Skill: Long *o* (CVC*e*)

Cole	hope	Poke	Rose
home	joke	rope	woke

Previously Taught Skills

a	day	is	on	take
and	dog	it	pal	time
at	fast	Jake	pals	trick
best	get	kick	play	tricks
big	has	let	put	up
block	hat	like	run	win
can	his	Mom	spin	yes

SKILLS APPLIED IN WORDS IN STORY: short *a*; short *i*; short *o*; short *u*; short *e*; long *a* (CVC*e*); long *i* (CVC*e*); /k/ spelled *c*; long *o* (CVC*e*) **From Grade 1:** consonants; short vowels; initial and final blends; long *a* spelled *ay*; /k/ spelled *ck*; /z/ spelled *s*; inflection -*s*

HIGH-FREQUENCY WORDS

a	family	said	to	with
be	go	school	today	
do	I	so	try	
does	now	the	will	

Houghton Mifflin Harcourt.

Cole Woke Up

High-Frequency Words Taught to Date

Grade 1	brown	far	here	myself	right	those	would
a	buy	father	high	near	said	thought	write
about	by	few	hold	never	school	three	years
above	call	field	house	new	second	to	yellow
across	car	find	how	night	see	today	you
after	carry	first	I	no	seven	together	young
again	caught	five	idea	noise	shall	too	your
all	city	fly	into	nothing	she	took	
almost	cold	follow	is	now	should	toward	*Grade 2*
along	come	food	kinds	of	show	try	cheer
always	could	for	know	off	sing	two	children
and	country	four	large	old	small	under	hello
animal	covers	friend	laugh	once	soil	until	hundred
are	cried	friendship	learning	one	some	use	mind
around	different	full	light	only	sometimes	very	next
away	do	funny	like	open	soon	walk	other
baby	does	give	listen	or	sorry	want	this
ball	done	go	little	our	starts	warms	
be	don't	goes	live	out	stories	was	
bear	door	good	long	over	story	wash	
beautiful	down	great	look	own	studied	watch	
because	draw	green	loudly	paper	sure	water	
been	earth	ground	loved	party	surprised	we	
before	eat	grow	make	people	take	were	
began	eight	happy	many	pictures	talk	what	
begins	enough	have	maybe	play	teacher	where	
bird	even	he	me	please	the	who	
blue	every	head	minute	pull	their	why	
both	everyone	hear	more	pushed	there	window	
boy	eyes	heard	most	put	these	with	
bring	fall	help	mother	read	they	work	
brothers	family	her	my	ready	think	world	

Decoding skills taught to date: short *a*; short *i*; short *o*; short *u*; short *e*; closed syllables; long *a* (CVC*e*); long *i* (CVC*e*); /k/ spelled *c*; /s/ spelled *c*; long *o* (CVCe)   **From Grade 1**: consonants; short vowels; initial and final blends; long *a* spelled *ay*; /k/ spelled *ck*; /z/ spelled *s*; inflection *-s*

Cole Woke Up

Mom said, "Get up, Cole!"

Cole woke up. Mom said, "Today will be the best day."

Cole said, "I hope so, Mom."

"It is a school day," said Mom.

"Yes!" said Cole.

1

Cole can play with his pals Rose and Jake. Cole can spin his rope and do tricks. Rose and Jake like the tricks Cole does with the rope. Will Cole let his pals take his rope to try to do a trick?

4

Cole can play with his pals at school.
Cole can kick, block, kick. Cole can run
fast. Cole can win! Yes, Cole!
Now, it is time to go home.

Cole can play at home. His family
has a dog, Poke, at home. Cole can joke
with Poke. Cole can put a big hat on
Poke. Poke is his best pal.

Big Ice Cubes

DECODABLE WORDS

Target Skill: **long *u* /yōō/ (CVC*e*)**

cubes   mules   used

Previously Taught Skills

an	freezers	in	packed	that
at	froze	it	past	them
big	get	lake	path	this
box	got	lakes	piles	time
but	had	long	poles	tired
came	home	made	sawdust	way
carts	homes	make	sell	when
cut	hot	man	stacked	wide
days	ice	men	stay	with
did	icemen	not	take	

SKILLS APPLIED IN WORDS IN STORY: short *a*; short *i*; CVC syllable pattern; short *o*; short *u*; short *e*; long *a* (CVC*e*); long *i* (CVC*e*); /k/ spelled *c*; /s/ spelled *c*; long *o* (CVC*e*), long *u* /yōō/   **From Grade 1:** consonants; short vowels; base words and ending -*ed* /d/; long *a* spelled *ai* and *ay*; long *e* (*e*, *ee*), consonants -*ck*; final blends *st*; *r*-controlled vowel *ar*; digraph *th*; digraph *wh*; vowel combinations *aw, au*

HIGH-FREQUENCY WORDS

a	cold	house	people	to
and	for	of	the	was
away	have	out	they	were

Houghton Mifflin Harcourt.

© Houghton Mifflin Harcourt Publishing Company

BOOK 25

Big Ice Cubes

June plays "June's Tune" and "The Big Tune" for Mom and Dad. They like "June's Tune" best. June plays it at the flute show. People clap and clap for June's tune. But no one can sing like Luke can.

4

June's Flute

June is six. June has a dog, Luke. June has a flute. June likes to play tunes on her flute for Luke.

1

June plays the flute a lot. She likes to play "June's Tune." It is a fun tune! June likes to play "The Big Tune." Luke sings with June when she plays tunes.

June can be in a flute show. June will pick a nice tune to play on her flute. Will June play "June's Tune"? Will June play "The Big Tune"? Luke likes June's tunes.

It Is June

DECODABLE WORDS

Target Skill: **long *u* /ōō/ (CVC*e*)**

Bruce	June	prune	tunes
cute	Luke	spruce	
Duke	Luke's	tube	

Previously Taught Skills

as	help	it	pup	we
can	helped	me	sing	will
first	his	Mom	this	
game	is	picked	up	

SKILLS APPLIED IN WORDS IN STORY: short *a*; short *i*; short *o*; short *u*; short *e*; long *a* (CVC*e*); /k/ spelled *c*; /s/ spelled *c*; long *u* /ōō/ (CVC*e*) **From Grade 1:** consonants; short vowels; /z/ spelled *s*; final consonants *ll*; final blend *st*; digraph *th*; ending *-ed* /d/; long *e* (*e*); final consonants *ng*; r-controlled *ir*

HIGH-FREQUENCY WORDS

a	every	I	too
blue	few	said	you
called	house	the	

▲●○ **Houghton Mifflin Harcourt**

It Is June

High-Frequency Words Taught to Date

Grade 1

a	brothers	fall	heard	more	pull	the	where
about	brown	family	help	most	pushed	their	who
above	buy	far	her	mother	put	there	why
across	by	father	here	my	read	these	window
after	call	few	high	myself	ready	they	with
again	car	field	hold	near	right	think	work
all	carry	find	house	never	said	those	world
almost	caught	first	how	new	school	thought	would
along	city	five	I	night	second	three	write
always	cold	fly	idea	no	see	to	years
and	come	follow	into	noise	seven	today	yellow
animal	could	food	is	nothing	shall	together	you
are	country	for	kinds	now	she	too	young
around	covers	four	know	of	should	took	your
away	cried	friend	large	off	show	toward	
baby	different	friendship	laugh	old	sing	try	**Grade 2**
ball	do	full	learning	once	small	two	cheer
be	does	funny	light	one	soil	under	children
bear	done	give	like	only	some	until	hello
beautiful	don't	go	listen	open	sometimes	use	hundred
because	door	goes	little	or	soon	very	mind
been	down	good	live	our	sorry	walk	next
before	draw	great	long	out	starts	want	other
began	earth	green	look	over	stories	warms	this
begins	eat	ground	loudly	own	story	was	
bird	eight	grow	loved	paper	studied	wash	
blue	enough	happy	make	party	sure	watch	
both	even	have	many	people	surprised	water	
boy	every	he	maybe	pictures	take	we	
bring	everyone	head	me	play	talk	were	
	eyes	hear	minute	please	teacher	what	

Decoding skills taught to date: short *a*; short *i*; closed syllables (CVC); short *o*; short *u*; short *e*; long *a* (CVC*e*); long *i* (CVC*e*); /k/ spelled *c*; /s/ spelled *c*; long *o* (CVC*e*); long *u* /yōō/ (CVC*e*); long *u* /ōō/ (CVC*e*)

"I will prune this blue spruce,"
said Bruce.

"As I prune, I will sing a few tunes!"

Luke picked up his tube game. Luke's
cute pup, Duke, helped, too!

2

3

Eve said, "I can see a hole in the hill. Will it fit Zeke?"

It will fit Zeke! Zeke is stuck! Eve and Pete tug, tug, tug Zeke. Zeke is glad. He wags, wags, wags.

Then Zeke, Eve, and Pete run fast, fast, fast back down the hill.

4

Pete, Eve, and Zeke

Pete and Eve hike up the hill. They take their dog, Zeke. Zeke runs up the hill fast, fast, fast. Then he runs back to Pete and Eve.

The hill is tall. Pete and Eve can not run fast. Then Pete, Eve, and Zeke get to the hilltop.

1

© Houghton Mifflin Harcourt Publishing Company

Pete and Eve sit on the grass. They can see far.

"I can see a bus," said Pete.

"I can see a flag," said Eve.

Then Pete said, "I can hear Zeke, but I can not see Zeke."

Pete calls, "Zeke! Zeke! Zeke!"

Eve calls, "Zeke! Zeke! Zeke!"

Big, Big Rig

DECODABLE WORDS

Target Skill: /g/ spelled *g*

big	get	go	Meg	rig

Previously Taught Skills

and	fine	in	ride	take
belts	hats	is	rides	up
can	helps	next	safe	will
Dad	his	on	sit	

SKILLS APPLIED IN WORDS IN STORY: short *a*; short *i*; short *o*; short *u*; short *e*;
long *a* (CVCe); long *i* (CVCe); /k/ spelled *c*; /g/ spelled *g*   **From Grade 1:** consonants; short
vowels; /z/ spelled *s*; inflection -*s*; final consonants *ll*; final blend *nd*; ending -*s*; long *o* (CV)

HIGH-FREQUENCY WORDS

a	look	they	where
are	the	to	with

Houghton Mifflin Harcourt.

Big, Big Rig

It Is June

"We can spruce up every June!"
said Mom.

"Bruce! Luke!" called Mom.
"It is June first! Will you help me
spruce up the house?"

4

1

High-Frequency Words Taught to Date

Grade 1	brown	far	here	myself	right	those	would
a	buy	father	high	near	said	thought	write
about	by	few	hold	never	school	three	years
above	call	field	house	new	second	to	yellow
across	car	find	how	night	see	today	you
after	carry	first	I	no	seven	together	young
again	caught	five	idea	noise	shall	too	your
all	city	fly	into	nothing	she	took	
almost	cold	follow	is	now	should	toward	Grade 2
along	come	food	kinds	of	show	try	cheer
always	could	for	know	off	sing	two	children
and	country	four	large	old	small	under	hello
animal	covers	friend	laugh	once	soil	until	hundred
are	cried	friendship	learning	one	some	use	mind
around	different	full	light	only	sometimes	very	next
away	do	funny	like	open	soon	walk	other
baby	does	give	listen	or	sorry	want	this
ball	done	go	little	our	starts	warms	
be	don't	goes	live	out	stories	was	
bear	door	good	long	over	story	wash	
beautiful	down	great	look	own	studied	watch	
because	draw	green	loudly	paper	sure	water	
been	earth	ground	loved	party	surprised	we	
before	eat	grow	make	people	take	were	
began	eight	happy	many	pictures	talk	what	
begins	enough	have	maybe	play	teacher	where	
bird	even	he	me	please	the	who	
blue	every	head	minute	pull	their	why	
both	everyone	hear	more	pushed	there	window	
boy	eyes	heard	most	put	these	with	
bring	fall	help	mother	read	they	work	
brothers	family	her	my	ready	think	world	

Decoding skills taught to date: short *a*; short *i*; closed syllables (CVC); short *o*; short *u*; short *e*; long *a* (CVC*e*); long *i* (CVC*e*); /k/ spelled *c*; /s/ spelled *c*; long *o* (CVC*e*); long *u* /yo͞o/ (CVC*e*); long *u* /o͞o/ (CVC*e*); long *e* (CVC*e*); /g/ spelled *g*

Go, big, big rig! Where will the big
rig go? The big rig will take Meg and
Dad on a fine ride. Go, big, big rig!
Go!

Big, Big Rig

Look at Meg and Dad. Meg helps
Dad on his rig. Dad rides a big, big rig.
Meg rides next to Dad.

© Houghton Mifflin Harcourt Publishing Company

Meg and Dad can go in the big, big rig. Dad helps Meg get up. Meg is safe with Dad.

Meg and Dad sit in the big, big rig. They are safe with belts and hats. Where will Meg and Dad go in the big, big rig?

Here, Rex!

DECODABLE WORDS

Target Skill: /g/ spelled *g*

bag	dog	get	Meg's
beg	Gabe	Meg	

Previously Taught Skills

and	bite	it	not	smile
at	bites	like	Rex	stop
back	can	mad	runs	will
bib	has	must	sat	
bit	is	named	save	

SKILLS APPLIED IN WORDS IN STORY: short *a*; short *i*; short *o*; short *u*; short *e*; long *a* (CVCe); long *i* (CVCe); /k/ spelled *c*; /g/ spelled *g* **From Grade 1:** consonants; short vowels; /z/ spelled *s*; inflection *-s*; final consonants *ll*; consonants *-ck*; blends with *s*; final blend *st*; ending *-s*; ending *-ed* /d/; possessives with *'s*

HIGH-FREQUENCY WORDS

a	happy	they
are	here	to
do	now	what

Houghton Mifflin Harcourt

Here, Rex!

Page and Smudge

"Smudge! Smudge!" Page yelled as she went on the bridge. Then she saw her dog, Smudge, in a hedge. Page ran to the hedge. Smudge was wedged in by the hedge and the lodge.

"Page, try to budge Smudge now," Mom said. Then Smudge budged!

"Now we are smudged with mud!" said Mom.

"And Smudge is wet!" said Page.

Page nudged Smudge, but Smudge
did not budge. Smudge was stuck!

Then Page saw Mom at the edge of
the bridge. Page yelled, "Mom, Smudge
is stuck and will not budge!"

Page and Mom nudged Smudge.
Smudge still did not budge!

Mom ran back to the bridge. Then
she came back with a can of water.

"We can try this," Mom said. She
spilled water around Smudge. Smudge
dodged the water, but Smudge still did
not budge.

"Do not be sad," said Mom. "We will
get Smudge out!"

Greg Gets a Pet

DECODABLE WORDS

Target Skill: **blends with** *r*

branch	brown	Fran's	grass
brand	crate	from	Greg
brick	Fran	grand	grin
Brin	Frank's	grant	tracks

Previously Taught Skills

and	get	it	played	with
asked	gets	just	shop	yes
big	got	Mom	smiled	up
came	had	name	spot	visit
can	home	next	take	we
dog	I	pet	that	went
fun	is	picked	wish	will

SKILLS APPLIED IN WORDS IN STORY: short *a*; short *i*; closed syllables (CVC: short *a, i*); short *o*; short *u*; short *e*; closed syllables (CVC: short *o, u, e*); long *a* (CVCe); long *i* (CVCe); /k/ spelled *c*; long *o* (CVCe); consonant *g* (hard *g*); blends with *r*   **From Grade 1:** consonants; short vowels; words with *oa, ow*; inflection -*s*; final consonants *ll, ss*; consonants *ck*; final blends *nt, nd, xt*; digraphs *th, ch, sh*; ending -*ed*; possessives with '*s*; blends with *s, l*; words with *ai, ay*

HIGH-FREQUENCY WORDS

a	my	the
for	new	to
house	said	what

 Houghton Mifflin Harcourt.

Greg Gets a Pet

High-Frequency Words Taught to Date

Grade 1							
a	brothers	fall	heard	more	pull	the	where
about	brown	family	help	most	pushed	their	who
above	buy	far	her	mother	put	there	why
across	by	father	here	my	read	these	window
after	call	few	high	myself	ready	they	with
again	car	field	hold	near	right	think	work
all	carry	find	house	never	said	those	world
almost	caught	first	how	new	school	thought	would
along	city	five	I	night	second	three	write
always	cold	fly	idea	no	see	to	years
and	come	follow	into	noise	seven	today	yellow
animal	could	food	is	nothing	shall	together	you
are	country	for	kinds	now	she	too	young
around	covers	four	know	of	should	took	your
away	cried	friend	large	off	show	toward	
baby	different	friendship	laugh	old	sing	try	Grade 2
ball	do	full	learning	once	small	two	cheer
be	does	funny	light	one	soil	under	children
bear	done	give	like	only	some	until	hello
beautiful	don't	go	listen	open	sometimes	use	hundred
because	door	goes	little	or	soon	very	mind
been	down	good	live	our	sorry	walk	next
before	draw	great	long	out	starts	want	other
began	earth	green	look	over	stories	warms	says
begins	eat	ground	loudly	own	story	was	table
bird	eight	grow	loved	paper	studied	wash	this
blue	enough	happy	make	party	sure	watch	
both	even	have	many	people	surprised	water	
boy	every	he	maybe	pictures	take	we	
bring	everyone	head	me	play	talk	were	
	eyes	hear	minute	please	teacher	what	

Decoding skills taught to date: short *a*; short *i*; closed syllables (CVC: short *a*, *i*); short *o*; short *u*; short *e*; closed syllables (CVC: short *o*, *u*, *e*); long *a* (CVC*e*); long *i* (CVC*e*); /k/ spelled *c*; /s/ spelled *c*; long *o* (CVC*e*); long *u* /yo͞o/ (CVC*e*); long *u* /o͞o/ (CVC*e*); long *e* (CVC*e*); consonant *g* (hard *g*); /j/ spelled *g*, *dge*; blends with *r*

"Can I take Brin to Fran's house?" asked Greg. "Yes," said Mom.

Greg went to visit Fran. Greg picked up a branch from the grass. Fran and Greg played with Brin.

Brin, Fran, and Greg had fun! Brin is just the dog for Greg!

© Houghton Mifflin Harcourt Publishing Company

Greg Gets a Pet

Greg came home and said, "Mom, I had a grand wish. Can we get a brand new pet?"

"Greg, that is a wish I can grant. What pet will we get?" asked Mom.

"A big brown dog!" said Greg.

Mom and Greg went to Frank's Pet Shop. It is a brick shop next to the tracks.

Greg smiled and said, "I spot a grand dog! I will name my dog Brin!"
Mom and Greg got a crate to take Brin home. Greg had a big grin.

Drips and Drops on Gran

DECODABLE WORDS

Target Skill: blends with *r*

brim	drop	from	grins	trek
drip	drops	grabs	grips	
drips	frog	Gran	track	

Previously Taught Skills

and	big	hops	it	stops
at	hat	in	on	wet
bag	her	is	see	

SKILLS APPLIED IN WORDS IN STORY: short *a*; short *i*; closed syllables (CVC: short *a, i*); short *o*; short *u*; short *e*; closed syllables (CVC: short *o, u, e*); consonant *g* (hard *g*); blends with *r, s* **From Grade 1:** consonants; short vowels; /z/ spelled *s*; inflection *-s*; consonants *ck*; long *e* (*e, ee*); *r*-controlled *er*

HIGH-FREQUENCY WORDS

a	said	the
I	she	to
rain	starts	

Drips and Drops on Gran

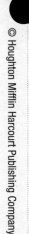

The flock can quack and flap
and cluck.

Quack, flap, cluck!

4

Quack, Flap, Cluck

Ducks in the flock flap.
Flap, flap, flap.

1

Ducks in the flock have flat bills.

Ducks in the flock quack.

Flap, quack. Flap, quack. Cluck.

© Houghton Mifflin Harcourt Publishing Company

Cluck, cluck, cluck.

Ducks quack. Ducks do not cluck.

A hen in the flock clucks!

Camp Sky

DECODABLE WORDS

Target Skill: blends with *s*

best	skit	snacks	Stan	Stef
mask	sky	sports	stand	step
scarf	sleep	stage	stars	stops
Skip	small	stamp	start	swim

Previously Taught Skills

and	gets	like	see	we
camp	he	lots	sees	when
can	his	make	short	
clap	home	note	tells	
dad	is	on	then	
for	it	pals	under	
fun	kids	play	up	

SKILLS APPLIED IN WORDS IN STORY: short *a*; short *i*; short *o*; short *u*; short *e*; CVC closed syllables; long *a* (CVCe); long *i* (CVCe); /k/ spelled *c*; long *o* (CVCe); /g/ spelled *g*; /j/ spelled *g*; blends with *l*; blends with *s*   **From Grade 1:** consonants; short vowels; /z/ spelled *s*; double final consonants: *ll*; consonants -*ck*; final blends: *mp*, *nd*; digraph *th*; base words and ending -*s*; digraph *sh*, *wh*; long *e* (*e*, *ee*); long *a* spelled *y*, *ai* and *ay*; *r*-controlled vowel *ar*; *r*-controlled vowel *or* and *ore*; *r*-controlled vowel *er*, *ir*, and *ur*

HIGH-FREQUENCY WORDS

a	goes	I	the	what
about	have	of	they	writes
come	help	says	to	you

Houghton Mifflin Harcourt.

High-Frequency Words Taught to Date

Grade 1	brothers	fall	heard	more	pull	the	where
a	brown	family	help	most	pushed	their	who
about	buy	far	her	mother	put	there	why
above	by	father	here	my	read	these	window
across	call	few	high	myself	ready	they	with
after	car	field	hold	near	right	think	work
again	carry	find	house	never	said	those	world
all	caught	first	how	new	school	thought	would
almost	city	five	I	night	second	three	write
along	cold	fly	idea	no	see	to	years
always	come	follow	into	noise	seven	today	yellow
and	could	food	is	nothing	shall	together	you
animal	country	for	kinds	now	she	too	young
are	covers	four	know	of	should	took	your
around	cried	friend	large	off	show	toward	
away	different	friendship	laugh	old	sing	try	*Grade 2*
baby	do	full	learning	once	small	two	cheer
ball	does	funny	light	one	soil	under	children
be	done	give	like	only	some	until	hello
bear	don't	go	listen	open	sometimes	use	hundred
beautiful	door	goes	little	or	soon	very	mind
because	down	good	live	our	sorry	walk	next
been	draw	great	long	out	starts	want	other
before	earth	green	look	over	stories	warms	says
began	eat	ground	loudly	own	story	was	table
begins	eight	grow	loved	paper	studied	wash	this
bird	enough	happy	make	party	sure	watch	
blue	even	have	many	people	surprised	water	
both	every	he	maybe	pictures	take	we	
boy	everyone	head	me	play	talk	were	
bring	eyes	hear	minute	please	teacher	what	

Decoding skills taught to date: short *a*; short *i*; closed syllables (CVC: short *a, i*); short *o*; short *u*; short *e*; closed syllables (CVC: short *o, u, e*); long *a* (CVC*e*); long *i* (CVC*e*); /k/ spelled *c*; /s/ spelled *c*; long *o* (CVC*e*); long *u* /yo͞o/ (CVC*e*); long *u* /o͞o/ (CVC*e*); long *e* (CVC*e*); /g/ spelled *g*; /j/ spelled *g, dge*; blends with *r*; blends with *l*; blends with *s* **From Grade 1:** consonants; short vowels; /z/ spelled *s*; double final consonants: *ll*; consonants *-ck*; final blends *mp, nd*; digraph *th*; base words and ending *-s*; digraphs *sh, wh*; long *e* (*e, ee*); long *a* spelled *y, ai*, and *ay*; *r*-controlled vowel *ar*; *r*-controlled vowel *or* and *ore*; *r*-controlled vowel *er, ir*, and *ur*

Camp Sky

Stan writes a note home. He tells his dad about the skit. Stan gets a stamp for his note. Then Stan goes to sleep.

Stan goes to Camp Sky. He says it is the best camp! Stan can swim and play sports. He can have snacks. Stan can sleep under the stars!

Stan sees his pals, Skip and Stef.

"Can we make up a skit?" says Skip.
"A skit is like a short play."

Stan says, "What fun! Can I help you
make a stage?"

Lots of kids see the skit. Stan, Skip,
and Stef have a scarf and a small mask.
They step on the stage and start. When
the skit stops, kids stand and clap!

2

3

© Houghton Mifflin Harcourt Publishing Company

Stan's Sled

DECODABLE WORDS

Target Skill: **blends with *s***

sled	slides	speeds	Stan's	stuck
slick	smiles	spot	steep	
slide	snow	Stan	still	

Previously Taught Skills

and	has	his	on
can	he	is	sees
flat	hill	not	will

SKILLS APPLIED IN WORDS IN STORY: short *a*; short *i*; closed syllables (CVC: short *a, i*); short *o*; short *u*; short *e*; closed syllables (CVC: short *o, u, e*); long *i* (CVC*e*); blends with *l*; blends with *s*   **From Grade 1:** consonants; short vowels; /z/ spelled *s*; inflection -*s*; final consonants *ll*; possessives with *'s*; consonants *ck*; long *e* (*e, ee*); long *o* (*oa, ow*); final blend *nd*

HIGH-FREQUENCY WORDS

a

now

the

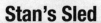
Houghton Mifflin Harcourt

Stan's Sled

The men get the net and find a rock.
Then the men can stand in the wind and
mend, mend, mend.

Stand and Mend

These men stand in the sand and
mend fishing nets.

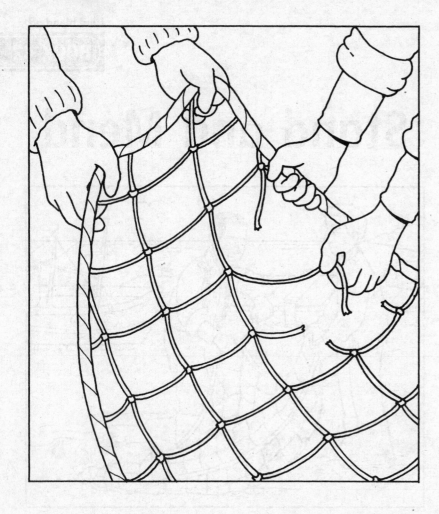

Nets can have cut strands. The men must mend cut strands with their hands.

Wind whips the net.
"Lend a hand!" yells the blond man.

Pang Wong's Loud House

DECODABLE WORDS

Target Skill: **final blend** *ng*

bong(s)	gong	Pang	songbird
bring	Ling	sing	Wong
clang(s)	Ming	song(s)	Wong's

Previously Taught Skills

and	he	next	that
back	hear	not	then
can	hit	now	this
Chin	home	or	took
cooking	house	pans	went
cooks	is	see	when
day	it	she	wife
did	loud	smiled	will
filled	makes	sound	wise
for	me	take	with

SKILLS APPLIED IN WORDS IN STORY: short *a*; short *i*; CVC syllable pattern; short *e*; long *a* (CVC); long *i* (CVC); /k/ spelled *c*; blends with *r*; blends with *s;* final blend *nd*; final blend *ng*   **From Grade 1:** consonants; short vowels; /z/ spelled *s*; double consonants *ll;* consonants -*ck;* final blend -*nt*; base words ending -*s*; base words ending -*ed* /d/; base words ending -*ing*; digraphs *th, ch, sh, wh*; long *e* (*e, ee*); long *e* (*ea, e_e*); compound words; *r*-controlled *or* and *ore*; vowel digraphs *oo* /o͞o/; vowel combinations *ou, ow*; long *e* spelled *y;* long *a* (*ay*); long *o* (CV)

HIGH-FREQUENCY WORDS

a	of	the	what
do	only	to	you
I	said	too	your
my	so	was	

Houghton Mifflin Harcourt.

Pang Wong's Loud House

High-Frequency Words Taught to Date

Grade 1

a	brothers	fall	heard	more	pull	the	where
about	brown	family	help	most	pushed	their	who
above	buy	far	her	mother	put	there	why
across	by	father	here	my	read	these	window
after	call	few	high	myself	ready	they	with
again	car	field	hold	near	right	think	work
all	carry	find	house	never	said	those	world
almost	caught	first	how	new	school	thought	would
along	city	five	I	night	second	three	write
always	cold	fly	idea	no	see	to	years
and	come	follow	into	noise	seven	today	yellow
animal	could	food	is	nothing	shall	together	you
are	country	for	kinds	now	she	too	young
around	covers	four	know	of	should	took	your
away	cried	friend	large	off	show	toward	
baby	different	friendship	laugh	old	sing	try	**Grade 2**
ball	do	full	learning	once	small	two	cheer
be	does	funny	light	one	soil	under	children
bear	done	give	like	only	some	until	hello
beautiful	don't	go	listen	open	sometimes	use	hundred
because	door	goes	little	or	soon	very	mind
been	down	good	live	our	sorry	walk	next
before	draw	great	long	out	starts	want	other
began	earth	green	look	over	stories	warms	says
begins	eat	ground	loudly	own	story	was	sleep
bird	eight	grow	loved	paper	studied	wash	table
blue	enough	happy	make	party	sure	watch	this
both	even	have	many	people	surprised	water	
boy	every	he	maybe	pictures	take	we	
bring	everyone	head	me	play	talk	were	
	eyes	hear	minute	please	teacher	what	

Decoding skills taught to date: short *a*; short *i*; closed syllables (CVC: short *a, i*); short *o*; short *u*; short *e*; closed syllables (CVC: short *o, u, e*); long *a* (CVC*e*); long *i* (CVC*e*); /k/ spelled *c*; /s/ spelled *c*; long *o* (CVC*e*); long *u* /yo͞o/ (CVC*e*); long *u* /o͞o/ (CVC*e*); long *e* (CVC*e*); /g/ spelled *g*; /j/ spelled *g, dge*; blends with *r*; blends with *l*; blends with *s*; final blend *nd*; final blend *ng*

Pang Wong's Loud House

Pang Wong went to see Wise Ming Chin. He said, "Wise Ming Chin, my house is too loud. My wife, Ling Wong, clangs the pans when she cooks. What can I do?"

Wise Ming Chin smiled and said, "Take this gong to your house. Hit it so that it makes a loud bong."

Pang Wong took the gong and the songbird back to Wise Ming Chin. Then he went home. He did not hear gong bongs or songbird songs. The only sound was the clang of cooking pans. Ling Wong smiled and said, "Pang Wong, now your house is not so loud!"

4

1

The next day, Pang Wong went back to Wise Ming Chin. He said, "Wise Ming Chin! Now my house is filled with pan clangs and gong bongs. It is too loud! What can I do?"

Wise Ming Chin smiled and said, "Take this songbird to your house. It will sing a song for you."

The next day, Pang Wong went back to Wise Ming Chin. He said, "Now my house is filled with pan clangs, gong bongs, and songbird songs. It is too loud! What can I do?"

Wise Ming Chin smiled and said, "Bring the gong and songbird back to me, Pang Wong."

A Big Gong

DECODABLE WORDS

Target Skill: final blend *ng*

Bing	bring	King	ring	sing
bong	gong	rang	sang	songs

Previously Taught Skills

am	dad	is	not	will
and	did	man	sleeps	
bed	dreams	me	still	
bells	hit	Meg	up	
big	in	Meg's	wake	

SKILLS APPLIED IN WORDS IN STORY: short *a*; short *i*; closed syllables (CVC: short *a, i*); short *o*; short *u*; short *e*; closed syllables (CVC: short *o, u, e*); long *a* (CVCe); /g/ spelled *g*; blends with *r*; blends with *l*; blends with *s*; final blend *ng*   **From Grade 1:** consonants; short vowels; possessives with '*s*; long vowel spelling patterns for *a, e, i, o, u*

HIGH-FREQUENCY WORDS

a	near	the
I	said	

 Houghton Mifflin Harcourt.

A Big Gong

High-Frequency Words Taught to Date

Grade 1							
a	brothers	fall	heard	more	pull	the	where
about	brown	family	help	most	pushed	their	who
above	buy	far	her	mother	put	there	why
across	by	father	here	my	read	these	window
after	call	few	high	myself	ready	they	with
again	car	field	hold	near	right	think	work
all	carry	find	house	never	said	those	world
almost	caught	first	how	new	school	thought	would
along	city	five	I	night	second	three	write
always	cold	fly	idea	no	see	to	years
and	come	follow	into	noise	seven	today	yellow
animal	could	food	is	nothing	shall	together	you
are	country	for	kinds	now	she	too	young
around	covers	four	know	of	should	took	your
away	cried	friend	large	off	show	toward	
baby	different	friendship	laugh	old	sing	try	Grade 2
ball	do	full	learning	once	small	two	cheer
be	does	funny	light	one	soil	under	children
bear	done	give	like	only	some	until	hello
beautiful	don't	go	listen	open	sometimes	use	hundred
because	door	goes	little	or	soon	very	mind
been	down	good	live	our	sorry	walk	next
before	draw	great	long	out	starts	want	other
began	earth	green	look	over	stories	warms	says
begins	eat	ground	loudly	own	story	was	sleep
bird	eight	grow	loved	paper	studied	wash	table
blue	enough	happy	make	party	sure	watch	this
both	even	have	many	people	surprised	water	
boy	every	he	maybe	pictures	take	we	
bring	everyone	head	me	play	talk	were	
	eyes	hear	minute	please	teacher	what	

Decoding skills taught to date: short *a*; short *i*; closed syllables (CVC: short *a, i*); short *o*; short *u*; short *e*; closed syllables (CVC: short *o, u, e*); long *a* (CVC*e*); long *i* (CVC*e*); /k/ spelled *c*; /s/ spelled *c*; long *o* (CVC*e*); long *u* /yo͞o/ (CVC*e*); long *u* /o͞o/ (CVC*e*); long *e* (CVC*e*); /g/ spelled *g*; /j/ spelled *g, dge*; blends with *r*; blends with *l*; blends with *s*; final blend *nd*; final blend *ng*

King Bing hit the gong.
BONG! BONG! BONG!
"I am up! I am up, Dad!" said Meg.

4

A Big Gong

Meg is in bed. Meg sleeps and dreams. Meg's dad is King Bing.
"Wake up!" said King Bing. Meg did not wake up.

1

"Ring bells! Sing songs!" said King
Bing. A man near the king rang bells
and sang songs. Meg still did not wake
up.

"Meg will not wake up!" said
King Bing.
"Bring me the big gong!"

The Hidden Trunk

DECODABLE WORDS

Target Skill: **final blend** *nk*

bank	Franklin	pink	trunk
blink	hanky	sink	trunk's
clank	junk	thanks	yanked
dank	mink	think	

Previously Taught Skills

an	dusty	hat	made	stuff
and	empty	he	map	tell
basement	found	hidden	new	these
big	fun	in	nice	things
born	game	is	not	this
dad	gave	it	puff	up
dark	Gran	just	she	will
down	Granddad	lid	shut	with
dust	had	loud	sit	you

SKILLS APPLIED IN WORDS IN STORY: short *a*; short *i*; CVC syllable pattern (closed syllables); short *o*; short *u*; short *e*; long *a* (CVCe); /k/ spelled *c*; long *o* (CVCe); blends with *r*; blends with *l*; blends with *s*; final blend *nd*; final blend *nk*   **From Grade 1:** consonant sounds; /z/ spelled *s*; double final consonants *ff*, *ll*; final blend *nt*; digraphs *sh*, *th*; base words and ending *-ed* /d/, /t/; base words and ending *-ing*; possessives with '*s*; long *e* (*e*, *ee*); long *e* (*ea*, *e_e*); *r*-controlled *ar*, *or*; vowel digraph *oo* /o͞o/; vowel digraph /o͞o/ spelled *oo*, *ou*, *ew*; vowel combinations *ou*, *ow*; long *e* spelled *y*

HIGH-FREQUENCY WORDS

a	for	old	was
about	I	said	were
before	long	story	what
do	of	the	your

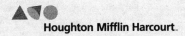

The Hidden Trunk

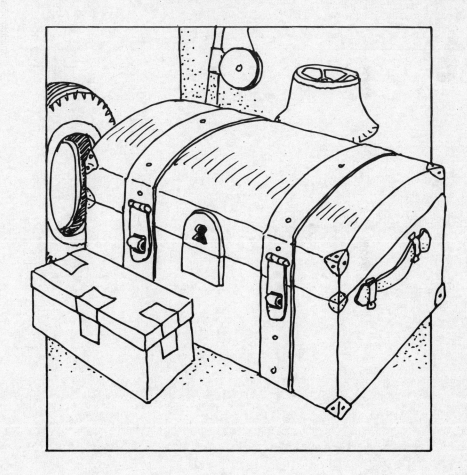

High-Frequency Words Taught to Date

Grade 1							
a	brothers	fall	heard	more	pull	teacher	what
about	brown	family	help	most	pushed	the	where
above	buy	far	her	mother	put	their	who
across	by	father	here	my	read	there	why
after	call	few	high	myself	ready	these	window
again	car	field	hold	near	right	they	with
all	carry	find	house	never	said	think	work
almost	caught	first	how	new	school	those	world
along	city	five	I	night	second	thought	would
always	cold	fly	idea	no	see	three	write
and	come	follow	into	noise	seven	to	years
animal	could	food	is	nothing	shall	today	yellow
are	country	for	kinds	now	she	together	you
around	covers	four	know	of	should	too	young
away	cried	friend	large	off	show	took	your
baby	different	friendship	laugh	old	sing	toward	
ball	do	full	learning	once	small	try	**Grade 2**
be	does	funny	light	one	soil	two	cheer
bear	done	give	like	only	some	under	children
beautiful	don't	go	listen	open	some-	until	hello
because	door	goes	little	or	times	use	hundred
been	down	good	live	our	soon	very	mind
before	draw	great	long	out	sorry	walk	next
began	earth	green	look	over	starts	want	other
begins	eat	ground	loudly	own	stories	warms	says
bird	eight	grow	loved	paper	story	was	sleep
blue	enough	happy	make	party	studied	wash	table
both	even	have	many	people	sure	watch	this
boy	every	he	maybe	pictures	surprised	water	
bring	everyone	head	me	play	take	we	
	eyes	hear	minute	please	talk	were	

Decoding skills taught to date: short *a*; short *i*; CVC syllable pattern (closed syllables); short o; short u; short e; long *a* (CVC*e*); long *i* (CVC*e*); /k/ spelled *c*; /s/ spelled *c*; long *o* (CVC*e*); long *u* /yōō/ (CVC*e*); long *u* /ōō/ (CVC*e*); long *e* (CVC*e*); /g/ spelled *g*; /j/ spelled *g*, *dge*; blends with *r*; blends with *l*; blends with *s*; final blend *nd*; final blend *ng*; final blend *nk*

"Franklin!" said Gran. "This stuff is not junk. Granddad and I had these things before your dad was born. Sit down, and I will tell you about this trunk."

"Nice! Thanks!" said Franklin.

4

The Hidden Trunk

Gran made up a fun new game. She gave Franklin a map. It had an "X."

"Find my hidden trunk, Franklin," said Gran. "Use the map."

1

Franklin found the trunk in the dark, dank basement. He yanked the trunk's lid. It made a loud clank. A puff of dust made Franklin blink.

What do you think Franklin found?

He found a pink hanky, an empty bank, a dusty mink hat, and an old sink. Franklin shut the trunk lid with a big clank. "This stuff is just junk," he said.

Thanks, Frank!

DECODABLE WORDS

Target Skill: **final blend** *nk*

blank	Hank	tank	thanks
Frank	ink	thank	trunk

Previously Taught Skills

and	got	then
fish	left	this
gave	page	will

SKILLS APPLIED IN WORDS IN STORY: short *a*; short *i*; closed syllables (CVC: short *a, i*); short *o*; short *u*; short *e*; closed syllables (CVC: short *o, u, e*); long *a* (CVCe); /g/ spelled *g*; /j/ spelled *g, dge*; blends with *r*; blends with *l*   **From Grade 1:** consonants; short vowels; /z/ spelled *s*; inflection *-s*; final consonants *ll*; digraph *th*; long *e* (*e, ee*)

HIGH-FREQUENCY WORDS

a	I	some	your
for	paper	the	
friend	said	you	

© Houghton Mifflin Harcourt Publishing Company

Thanks, Frank!

High-Frequency Words Taught to Date

Grade 1							
a	brothers	fall	heard	more	pull	the	where
about	brown	family	help	most	pushed	their	who
above	buy	far	her	mother	put	there	why
across	by	father	here	my	read	these	window
after	call	few	high	myself	ready	they	with
again	car	field	hold	near	right	think	work
all	carry	find	house	never	said	those	world
almost	caught	first	how	new	school	thought	would
along	city	five	I	night	second	three	write
always	cold	fly	idea	no	see	to	years
and	come	follow	into	noise	seven	today	yellow
animal	could	food	is	nothing	shall	together	you
are	country	for	kinds	now	she	too	young
around	covers	four	know	of	should	took	your
away	cried	friend	large	off	show	toward	
baby	different	friendship	laugh	old	sing	try	**Grade 2**
ball	do	full	learning	once	small	two	cheer
be	does	funny	light	one	soil	under	children
bear	done	give	like	only	some	until	hello
beautiful	don't	go	listen	open	sometimes	use	hundred
because	door	goes	little	or	soon	very	mind
been	down	good	live	our	sorry	walk	next
before	draw	great	long	out	starts	want	other
began	earth	green	look	over	stories	warms	says
begins	eat	ground	loudly	own	story	was	sleep
bird	eight	grow	loved	paper	studied	wash	table
blue	enough	happy	make	party	sure	watch	this
both	even	have	many	people	surprised	water	
boy	every	he	maybe	pictures	take	we	
bring	everyone	head	me	play	talk	were	
	eyes	hear	minute	please	teacher	what	

Decoding skills taught to date: short *a*; short *i*; closed syllables (CVC: short *a, i*); short *o*; short *u*; short *e*; closed syllables (CVC: short *o, u, e*); long *a* (CVC*e*); long *i* (CVC*e*); /k/ spelled *c*; /s/ spelled *c*; long *o* (CVC*e*); long *u* /yo͞o/ (CVC*e*); long *u* /o͞o/ (CVC*e*); long *e* (CVC*e*); /g/ spelled *g*; /j/ spelled *g, dge*; blends with *r*; blends with *l*; blends with *s*; final blend *nd*; final blend *ng*; final blend *nk*

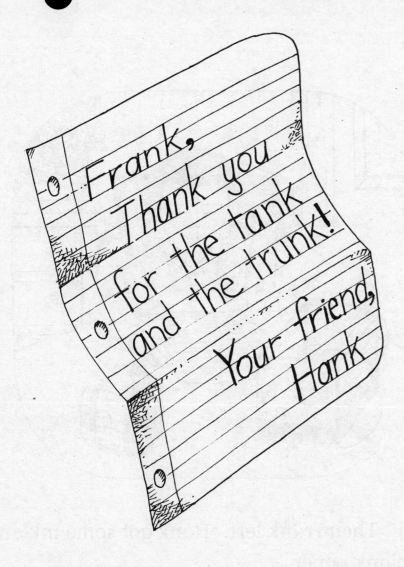

Hank gave Frank this page. "Thanks, Hank!" said Frank.

4

Thanks, Frank!

Frank gave Hank a fish tank. "Thanks, Frank!" said Hank.

1

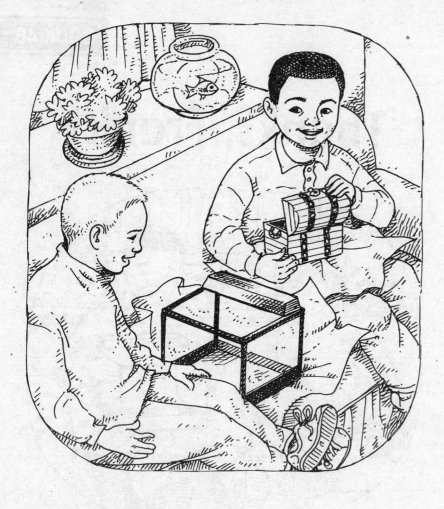

Frank gave Hank a trunk.
"Thanks, Frank!" said Hank.

Then Frank left. Hank got some ink and
blank paper.
"I will thank Frank," said Hank.

2

3

Trent Pretends

DECODABLE WORDS

Target Skill: **final blend *nt***

dentist	paints	pretends	Trent
glint	pretend	tent	

Previously Taught Skills

an	camps	is	smiles
and	days	makes	wet
art	his	must	with
artist	home	on	
camper	in	smile	

SKILLS APPLIED IN WORDS IN STORY: short *a*; short *i*; CVC syllable pattern (closed syllables); short *o*; short *u*; short *e*; long *a* (CVC*e*); long *i* (CVC*e*); /k/ spelled *c*; /g/ spelled *g*; blends with *r*; blends with *s*; blends with *l*; final blend *nd*; final blend *nt*   **From Grade 1:** consonants; short vowels; *r*-controlled *ar*; base words and ending *er*; base words and inflection *er*

HIGH-FREQUENCY WORDS

a	great	like	sure
does	he	play	to

Houghton Mifflin Harcourt.

Trent Pretends

Dell

Lill puts Dell in bed. Lill is glad that Dell is here.

See Lill and her doll, Dell. Dell is new. Dell is a pal.

Lill put Dell on a sill. Dell fell. Lill ran to help. Lill can get Dell well.

"You fell, Dell," said Lill. "This is not fun. You got a bad bump. I will help you get well, Dell."

Jill and Bill

DECODABLE WORDS

Target Skill: double final consonants *ll*

Bill	fill	hill	hills	Jill

Previously Taught Skills

and	dog	hot	pants	up
best	get	it	ran	
big	gets	lap	run	
can	has	likes	runs	
cup	help	pan	stop	

SKILLS APPLIED IN WORDS IN STORY: short *a*; short *i*; short *o*; short *u*; short *e*; closed syllables (CVC); /k/ spelled *c*; /g/ spelled *g*; final blend *nd*; final blend *nt*; double final consonants *ll* **From Grade 1:** consonants; short vowels; /z/ spelled *s*; inflection *-s*; final blend *st*; blends with *l*; blends with *s*

HIGH-FREQUENCY WORDS

a	friend	my	to
are	friend(s)	play	too
down	her	play(s)	we
for	I	said	with

Jill and Bill

Houghton Mifflin Harcourt

High-Frequency Words Taught to Date

Grade 1							
a	brothers	fall	heard	more	pull	the	where
about	brown	family	help	most	pushed	their	who
above	buy	far	her	mother	put	there	why
across	by	father	here	my	read	these	window
after	call	few	high	myself	ready	they	with
again	car	field	hold	near	right	think	work
all	carry	find	house	never	said	those	world
almost	caught	first	how	new	school	thought	would
along	city	five	I	night	second	three	write
always	cold	fly	idea	no	see	to	years
and	come	follow	into	noise	seven	today	yellow
animal	could	food	is	nothing	shall	together	you
are	country	for	kinds	now	she	too	young
around	covers	four	know	of	should	took	your
away	cried	friend	large	off	show	toward	
baby	different	friendship	laugh	old	sing	try	**Grade 2**
ball	do	full	learning	once	small	two	air
be	does	funny	light	one	soil	under	cheer
bear	done	give	like	only	some	until	children
beautiful	don't	go	listen	open	sometimes	use	hello
because	door	goes	little	or	soon	very	hundred
been	down	good	live	our	sorry	walk	mind
before	draw	great	long	out	starts	want	next
began	earth	green	look	over	stories	warms	other
begins	eat	ground	loudly	own	story	was	pretty
bird	eight	grow	loved	paper	studied	wash	says
blue	enough	happy	make	party	sure	watch	sleep
both	even	have	many	people	surprised	water	table
boy	every	he	maybe	pictures	take	we	this
bring	everyone	head	me	play	talk	were	told
	eyes	hear	minute	please	teacher	what	

Decoding skills taught to date: short *a*; short *i*; short *o*; short *u*; short *e*; closed syllables (CVC); long *a* (CVC*e*); long *i* (CVC*e*); /k/ spelled *c*; /s/ spelled *c*; long *o* (CVC*e*); long *u* /yōō/(CVC*e*); long *u* /ōō/ (CVC*e*); long *e* (CVC*e*); /g/ spelled *g*; /j/ spelled *g*, *dge*; blends with *r*; blends with *l*; blends with *s*; final blend *nd*; final blend *ng*; final blend *nk*; final blend *nt*; double final consonants *ll*   **From Grade 1:** consonants; short vowels; /z/ spelled *s*; inflection -*s*; final blend *st*; blends with *l*; blends with *s*

Jill and Bill

Jill has her dog, Bill. Jill and
Bill are best friends.

Jill and Bill ran down a big hill.

1

Jill can fill a pan for Bill. Jill
can fill a cup, too.

Jill said, "Bill can lap it up. I can
help my best friend, Bill."

4

Bill and the Bug

DECODABLE WORDS

Target Skill: **double final consonants *zz***

buzz	fuzz	razz

Previously Taught Skills

and	can	gets	is	not
ate	close	has	it	on
Bill	did	his	make	went
bug	food	in	mom	wings

SKILLS APPLIED IN WORDS IN STORY: short *a, i, o, u, e*; closed syllables (CVC); long *a* (CVC*e*); long *i* (CVC*e*); /k/ spelled *c*; /s/ spelled *c*; long *o* (CVC*e*); /g/ spelled *g*; blends with *l*; final blends *nd*; final blend *ng*; final blend *nt*; double final consonants *ll*; double final consonants *zz*   **From Grade 1:** consonants; short vowels; /z/ spelled *s*; inflection *-s*; ending *-s*; consonant digraph *th*

HIGH-FREQUENCY WORDS

a	hear	the
away	now	then
by	see	to

Bill and the Bug

High-Frequency Words Taught to Date

Grade 1	brown	far	here	myself	right	those	would
a	buy	father	high	near	said	thought	write
about	by	few	hold	never	school	three	years
above	call	field	house	new	second	to	yellow
across	car	find	how	night	see	today	you
after	carry	first	I	no	seven	together	young
again	caught	five	idea	noise	shall	too	your
all	city	fly	into	nothing	she	took	
almost	cold	follow	is	now	should	toward	Grade 2
along	come	food	kinds	of	show	try	air
always	could	for	know	off	sing	two	cheer
and	country	four	large	old	small	under	children
animal	covers	friend	laugh	once	soil	until	hello
are	cried	friendship	learning	one	some	use	hundred
around	different	full	light	only	sometimes	very	mind
away	do	funny	like	open	soon	walk	next
baby	does	give	listen	or	sorry	want	other
ball	done	go	little	our	starts	warms	pretty
be	don't	goes	live	out	stories	was	says
bear	door	good	long	over	story	wash	sleep
beautiful	down	great	look	own	studied	watch	table
because	draw	green	loudly	paper	sure	water	this
been	earth	ground	loved	party	surprised	we	told
before	eat	grow	make	people	take	were	
began	eight	happy	many	pictures	talk	what	
begins	enough	have	maybe	play	teacher	where	
bird	even	he	me	please	the	who	
blue	every	head	minute	pull	their	why	
both	everyone	hear	more	pushed	there	window	
boy	eyes	heard	most	put	these	with	
bring	fall	help	mother	read	they	work	
brothers	family	her	my	ready	think	world	

Decoding skills taught to date: short *a*; short *i*; short *o*; short *u*; short *e*; closed syllables (CVC); long *a* (CVC*e*); long *i* (CVC*e*); /k/ spelled *c*; /s/ spelled *c*; long *o* (CVC*e*); long *u* /yo͞o/ (CVC*e*); long *u* /o͞o/ (CVCe); long *e* (CVC*e*); /g/ spelled *g*; /j/ spelled *g, dge*; blends with *r*; blends with *l*; blends with *s*; final blend *nd*; final blend *ng*; final blend *nk*; final blend *nt*; double final consonants *ll*; double final consonants *ss*; double final consonants *zz*
From Grade 1: consonants; short vowels; /z/ spelled *s*; inflection *-s*; ending *-s*; consonant digraph *th*

Bill and the Bug

Bill can see a bug. It has wings. Wings
make the bug buzz.

The bug did not razz Bill and his
Mom. It ate, and then it went away.

4

1

Buzz! Buzz! The bug is by his mom.
Mom can hear it buzz.

Buzz! Buzz! The bug is close to Bill.
It gets in his food. Now Bill can see
fuzz on the bug.

© Houghton Mifflin Harcourt Publishing Company

Will and Jess Run Fast

DECODABLE WORDS

Target Skill: double final consonants *zz*

buzz	fizz	fuzz	whizz

Previously Taught Skills

am	get	hot	not	take
and	gets	ice	on	tells
as	glide	in	pal	time
best	grab	is	past	up
bug	grass	it	pop	van
but	has	Jess	run	will
can	he	just	runs	zooms
drink	hill	long	sells	
end	him	lost	stem	
fast	his	make	sure	

SKILLS APPLIED IN WORDS IN STORY: short *a*; short *i*; short *o*; short *u*; short *e*; closed syllables (CVC); long *a* (CVC*e*); long *i* (CVC*e*); /k/ spelled *c*; /s/ spelled *c*; /g/ spelled *g*; long *u* (CVC*e*); blends with *r*; blends with *l*; blends with *s*; final blend *nd*; final blends *ng*; final blend *nt*; double final consonants *ll*; double final consonants *ss*; double final consonants *zz* **From Grade 1:** consonants; short vowels; /z/ spelled *s*; inflection -*s*; final blend *st*; consonant digraph *wh*

HIGH-FREQUENCY WORDS

a	hear	said	their	you
air	I	see	they	
be	one	that	to	
before	of	the	too	

Will and Jess Run Fast

Houghton Mifflin Harcourt.

High-Frequency Words Taught to Date

Grade 1							
a	brown	far	here	myself	right	those	would
about	buy	father	high	near	said	thought	write
above	by	few	hold	never	school	three	years
across	call	field	house	new	second	to	yellow
after	car	find	how	night	see	today	you
again	carry	first	I	no	seven	together	young
all	caught	five	idea	noise	shall	too	your
almost	city	fly	into	nothing	she	took	
along	cold	follow	is	now	should	toward	**Grade 2**
always	come	food	kinds	of	show	try	air
and	could	for	know	off	sing	two	cheer
animal	country	four	large	old	small	under	children
are	covers	friend	laugh	once	soil	until	hello
around	cried	friendship	learning	one	some	use	hundred
away	different	full	light	only	sometimes	very	mind
baby	do	funny	like	open	soon	walk	next
ball	does	give	listen	or	sorry	want	other
be	done	go	little	our	starts	warms	pretty
bear	don't	goes	live	out	stories	was	says
beautiful	door	good	long	over	story	wash	sleep
because	down	great	look	own	studied	watch	table
been	draw	green	loudly	paper	sure	water	this
before	earth	ground	loved	party	surprised	we	told
began	eat	grow	make	people	take	were	
begins	eight	happy	many	pictures	talk	what	
bird	enough	have	maybe	play	teacher	where	
blue	even	he	me	please	the	who	
both	every	head	minute	pull	their	why	
boy	everyone	hear	more	pushed	there	window	
bring	eyes	heard	most	put	these	with	
brothers	fall	help	mother	read	they	work	
	family	her	my	ready	think	world	

Decoding skills taught to date: short *a*; short *i*; short *o*; short *u*; short *e*; closed syllables (CVC); long *a* (CVC*e*); long *i* (CVC*e*); /k/ spelled *c*; /s/ spelled *c*; long *o* (CVC*e*); long *u* /yo͞o/ (CVC*e*); long *u* /o͞o/ (CVCe); long *e* (CVC*e*); /g/ spelled *g*; /j/ spelled *g, dge*; blends with *r*; blends with *l*; blends with *s*; final blend *nd*; final blend *ng*; final blend *nk*; final blend *nt*; double final consonants *ll*; double final consonants *ss*; double final consonants *zz*
From Grade 1: consonants; short vowels; /z/ spelled *s*; inflection -*s*; final blend *st*; consonant digraph *wh*

Will and Jess can see a van. It sells pop that has fizz. Will and Jess can run fast to get pop and ice . . . But they will take their time to drink it!

Will and Jess Run Fast

Will can run fast. Will can hear a buzz as he runs up the hill. A bug zooms past him. "That bug is fast," said Will. "But it is not as fast as I am."

Will can whizz past the bug.

Will can see his best pal, Jess. "You sure can run fast, Will," said Jess. "But I am just as fast."

Will gets a long stem of grass. It has fuzz on one end. Will can make the fuzz glide in the hot air. Jess can grab the fuzz before it gets lost in the grass. Will tells Jess, "You can be fast, too."

Jeff and Ruff

DECODABLE WORDS

Target Skill: double final consonants *ff*

huff	Jeff	puff	Ruff

Previously Taught Skills

and	go	in	rest	use
bag	grass	is	sit	will
big	help	it	smell	with
but	hike	like	take	
can	hill	long	then	
dog	him	not	top	
doze	his	pole	up	

SKILLS APPLIED IN WORDS IN STORY: short *a*; short *i*; closed syllables (CVC); short *o*; short *u*; short *e*; long *a* (CVCe); long *i* (CVCe); /k/ spelled *c*; long *o* (CVCe); long *u* /yōō/ (CVCe); /g/ spelled *g*; blends with *r*; blends with *s*; final blend *nd*; final blend *ng*; double final consonants *ll*; double final consonants *ss*; double final consonants *ff* **From Grade 1:** consonants; short vowels; /z/ spelled *s*; final blend *st*; consonant digraph *th*; long *o* (CV)

HIGH-FREQUENCY WORDS

a	go	the	too
air	here	they	was
do	more	to	

Jeff and Ruff

High-Frequency Words Taught to Date

Grade 1							
a	brown	far	here	myself	right	those	would
about	buy	father	high	near	said	thought	write
above	by	few	hold	never	school	three	years
across	call	field	house	new	second	to	yellow
after	car	find	how	night	see	today	you
again	carry	first	I	no	seven	together	young
all	caught	five	idea	noise	shall	too	your
almost	city	fly	into	nothing	she	took	
along	cold	follow	is	now	should	toward	**Grade 2**
always	come	food	kinds	of	show	try	air
and	could	for	know	off	sing	two	cheer
animal	country	four	large	old	small	under	children
are	covers	friend	laugh	once	soil	until	hello
around	cried	friendship	learning	one	some	use	hundred
away	different	full	light	only	sometimes	very	mind
baby	do	funny	like	open	soon	walk	next
ball	does	give	listen	or	sorry	want	other
be	done	go	little	our	starts	warms	pretty
bear	don't	goes	live	out	stories	was	says
beautiful	door	good	long	over	story	wash	sleep
because	down	great	look	own	studied	watch	table
been	draw	green	loudly	paper	sure	water	this
before	earth	ground	loved	party	surprised	we	told
began	eat	grow	make	people	take	were	
begins	eight	happy	many	pictures	talk	what	
bird	enough	have	maybe	play	teacher	where	
blue	even	he	me	please	the	who	
both	every	head	minute	pull	their	why	
boy	everyone	hear	more	pushed	there	window	
bring	eyes	heard	most	put	these	with	
brothers	fall	help	mother	read	they	work	
	family	her	my	ready	think	world	

Decoding skills taught to date: short *a*; short *i*; closed syllables (CVC); short *o*; short *u*; short *e*; long *a* (CVC*e*); long *i* (CVC*e*); /k/ spelled *c*; /s/ spelled *c*; long *o* (CVC*e*); long *u* /yo͞o/ (CVC*e*); long *u* /o͞o/ (CVC*e*); long *e* (CVC*e*); /g/ spelled *g*; /j/ spelled *g, dge*; blends with *r*; blends with *l*; blends with *s*; final blend *nd*; final blend *ng*; final blend *nk*; final blend *nt*; double final consonants *ll*; double final consonants *ss*; double final consonants *zz*; double final consonants *ff*

Here is the top. Jeff and Ruff sit. Jeff and Ruff do not huff and puff. Jeff and Ruff doze and rest. It was a long hike, but Jeff and Ruff like to doze in the grass and smell the air.

4

Jeff and Ruff

Jeff is with his dog, Ruff. Jeff will go up a big hill. His dog, Ruff will go up, too. Jeff will take a pole and a bag.

1

Jeff and Ruff go up, up, up. They hike and hike. Jeff can use his pole to help him hike.

Jeff and Ruff go up, up, up. Jeff can not take it. They huff and puff. Then they hike more.

Jack and Rick got to feed the ducks.
The ducks can peck at the food. Peck,
peck, peck!

"I like hens!" said Rick.

"I like ducks!" said Jack.

4

Ducks and Hens Peck

Jack and Rick went to see ducks and
hens. Jack and Rick like hens. Jack
and Rick like ducks. Jack said, "If we
have luck, we will get to feed hens
and ducks!"

1

Jack and Rick went to see hens.
The hens like to peck. The hens went,
"Cluck, cluck, cluck!"

Jack and Rick went to see ducks.
One duck sat on a rock. The ducks
went, "Quack, quack, quack!"

Mack Packs His Backpack

DECODABLE WORDS

Target Skill: **consonants -ck**

back	backpacks	pack	socks
backpack	Mack	packs	

Previously Taught Skills

and	cap	his	next	will
at	Dad	in	on	with
bed	get	is	take	
bus	has	it	time	
can	helps	Matt	trip	

SKILLS APPLIED IN WORDS IN STORY: short *a*; short *i*; closed syllables (CVC); short *o*; short *u*; short *e*; long *a* (CVCe); long *i* (CVCe); /k/ spelled *c*; /g/ spelled *g*; blends with *r*; final blend *nd*; double final consonants *ll*; consonants -*ck* **From Grade 1:** consonants; short vowels; /z/ spelled *s*; inflection -*s*; consonant digraph *th*; ending -*s*; compound words

HIGH-FREQUENCY WORDS

a	go	the	too
also	have	their	where
are	ready	to	

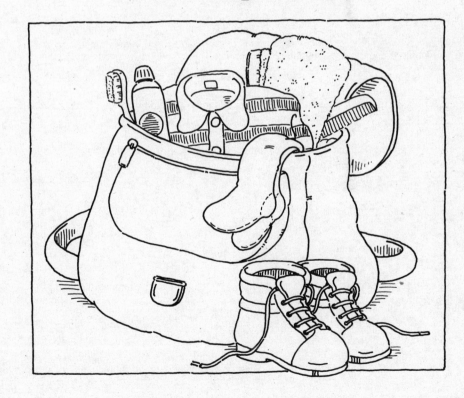

© Houghton Mifflin Harcourt Publishing Company

Mack Packs His Backpack

High-Frequency Words Taught to Date

Grade 1							
a	brown	far	here	myself	right	those	would
about	buy	father	high	near	said	thought	write
above	by	few	hold	never	school	three	years
across	call	field	house	new	second	to	yellow
after	car	find	how	night	see	today	you
again	carry	first	I	no	seven	together	young
all	caught	five	idea	noise	shall	too	your
almost	city	fly	into	nothing	she	took	
along	cold	follow	is	now	should	toward	*Grade 2*
always	come	food	kinds	of	show	try	air
and	could	for	know	off	sing	two	cheer
animal	country	four	large	old	small	under	children
are	covers	friend	laugh	once	soil	until	hello
around	cried	friendship	learning	one	some	use	hundred
away	different	full	light	only	sometimes	very	mind
baby	do	funny	like	open	soon	walk	next
ball	does	give	listen	or	sorry	want	other
be	done	go	little	our	starts	warms	pretty
bear	don't	goes	live	out	stories	was	says
beautiful	door	good	long	over	story	wash	sleep
because	down	great	look	own	studied	watch	table
been	draw	green	loudly	paper	sure	water	this
before	earth	ground	loved	party	surprised	we	told
began	eat	grow	make	people	take	were	
begins	eight	happy	many	pictures	talk	what	
bird	enough	have	maybe	play	teacher	where	
blue	even	he	me	please	the	who	
both	every	head	minute	pull*	their	why	
boy	everyone	hear	more	pushed	there	window	
bring	eyes	heard	most	put	these	with	
brothers	fall	help	mother	read	they	work	
	family	her	my	ready	think	world	

Decoding skills taught to date: short *a*; short *i*; closed syllables (CVC); short *o*; short *u*; short *e*; long *a* (CVC*e*); long *i* (CVC*e*); /k/ spelled *c*; /s/ spelled *c*; long *o* (CVC*e*); long *u* /yōō/ (CVC*e*); long *u* /ōō/ (CVC*e*); long *e* (CVC*e*); /g/ spelled *g*; /j/ spelled *g, dge*; blends with *r*; blends with *l*; blends with *s*; final blend *nd*; final blend *ng*; final blend *nk*; final blend *nt*; double final consonants *ll*; double final consonants *ss*; double final consonants *zz*; double final consonants *ff*; consonants *-ck*

Dad helps Matt get his backpack on his back. Mack has his backpack on his back, too. It is time to get on the bus. Where will Matt and Mack go?

Mack Packs His Backpack

Mack has his backpack on his bed. Matt will get ready. Mack will go on a trip. Matt will get ready. Mack can pack his socks. Next, Mack will pack a cap.

Mack and Matt are at the bus.
Matt has socks in his backpack, too.
Matt will also go on the trip. Matt will
go with Mack.

Matt and Mack will take the bus.
Matt and Mack have their backpack.
The socks are in the backpack, and
Matt and Mack are ready to go.

Shannon and Tanner

DECODABLE WORDS

Target Skill: double consonants (closed syllables)

borrow	lesson	puppets	Shannon
kitten	puppet	rabbit	Tanner

Previously Taught Skills

and	had	like	then
bag	hop	made	time
bed	in	make	tuck
can	is	Mom	we
for	it	morning	will
fun	jump	sing	yes
gave	kiss	skip	

SKILLS APPLIED IN WORDS IN STORY: short *a*; short *i*; closed syllables (CVC); short *o*; short *u*; short *e*; long *a* (CVCe); long *i* (CVCe); /k/ spelled *c*; long *e* (CVCe); /g/ spelled *g*; blends with *s*; final blend *nd*; final blend *ng*; double final consonants *ll*; double final consonants *ss*; consonants *-ck*; double consonants (closed syllables) **From Grade 1:** consonants; short vowels; inflection *-s*; consonant digraph *th*; long *e* (e); consonant digraph *sh*; long *o* (ow); r-controlled *or*; r-controlled *er*

HIGH-FREQUENCY WORDS

a	here	put	to
began	I	said	you
have	laugh	the	your

Shannon and Tanner

High-Frequency Words Taught to Date

Grade 1

a	brothers	fall	heard	more	pull	the	where
about	brown	family	help	most	pushed	their	who
above	buy	far	her	mother	put	there	why
across	by	father	here	my	read	these	window
after	call	few	high	myself	ready	they	with
again	car	field	hold	near	right	think	work
all	carry	find	house	never	said	those	world
almost	caught	first	how	new	school	thought	would
along	city	five	I	night	second	three	write
always	cold	fly	idea	no	see	to	years
and	come	follow	into	noise	seven	today	yellow
animal	could	food	is	nothing	shall	together	you
are	country	for	kinds	now	she	too	young
around	covers	four	know	of	should	took	your
away	cried	friend	large	off	show	toward	
baby	different	friendship	laugh	old	sing	try	*Grade 2*
ball	do	full	learning	once	small	two	air
be	does	funny	light	one	soil	under	cheer
bear	done	give	like	only	some	until	children
beautiful	don't	go	listen	open	sometimes	use	hello
because	door	goes	little	or	soon	very	hundred
been	down	good	live	our	sorry	walk	mind
before	draw	great	long	out	starts	want	next
began	earth	green	look	over	stories	warms	other
begins	eat	ground	loudly	own	story	was	pretty
bird	eight	grow	loved	paper	studied	wash	says
blue	enough	happy	make	party	sure	watch	sleep
both	even	have	many	people	surprised	water	table
boy	every	he	maybe	pictures	take	we	this
bring	everyone	head	me	play	talk	were	told
	eyes	hear	minute	please	teacher	what	

Decoding skills taught to date: short *a*; short *i*; closed syllables (CVC); short *o*; short *u*; short *e*; long *a* (CVC*e*); long *i* (CVC*e*); /k/ spelled *c*; /s/ spelled *c*; long *o* (CVC*e*); long *u* /yoo/ (CVC*e*); long *u* /oo/ (CVC*e*); long *e* (CVC*e*); /g/ spelled *g*, /j/ spelled *g*, *dge*; blends with *r*; blends with *l*; blends with *s*; final blend *nd*; final blend *ng*; final blend *nk*; final blend *nt*; double final consonants *ll*; double final consonants *ss*; double final consonants *zz*; double final consonants *ff*; consonants -*ck*; double consonants (closed syllables)

Shannon and Tanner

Then Mom said, "Shannon and Tanner, it is time for bed." Tanner and Shannon put the puppets in a bag.

Mom said, "I will tuck you in. Here is your kiss, Tanner. And here is your kiss, Shannon. We can have puppet fun in the morning!"

Shannon gave Tanner a lesson. "We will make a puppet," said Shannon.

"Yes," said Tanner. "I like puppets. I will make a rabbit puppet."

Shannon said, "And I will make a kitten puppet!"

Yikes! A moth is on the cloth.

The moth likes this cloth.

"I cannot get this top," said Bob.

"The moth ate a big hole in it!"

4

Moth on the Cloth

Bob is shopping for a top. Jill is helping him. Will Bob get this one?

"This cloth is thick. I do not like it," said Bob.

1

"Try this one," said Jill.

"This cloth is thin. It has a big rip. It does not fit! I cannot get this top," said Bob.

"Try this one," said Jill.

Will Bob get it?

"I like the cloth on this top the best," said Bob. "I will take it."

"It is a nice top," said Jill.

"I like it!" said Bob.

Swim and Swish

DECODABLE WORDS

Target Skill: **consonant digraph *sh***

fish	she	shore	swish
rush	shells	splash	Trish

Previously Taught Skills

and	deep	in	mask	thanks
as	feel	it	me	then
at	fins	kick	on	this
big	gets	lets	see	waves
can	got	like	swim	will
dad	helps	makes	swims	with

SKILLS APPLIED IN WORDS IN STORY: short *a*; short *i*; short *o*; short *u*; short *e*; CVC syllable pattern (closed syllables); long *a* (CVCe); long *i* (CVCe) /k/ spelled *c*; /g/ spelled *g*; blends with *r*; blends with *l*; blends with *s*; final blend *nd*; double final consonants *ll*; consonants *ck*; consonant digraph *th*; consonant digraph *sh* **From Grade 1:** consonants; short vowels; base words and ending *-s*; inflection *-s*; long *e* (*e, ee*); *r*-controlled vowel (*ore*)

HIGH-FREQUENCY WORDS

a	her	put	they
all	how	says	to
first	new	show	used
for	out	the	you

Houghton Mifflin Harcourt.

Swim and Swish

High-Frequency Words Taught to Date

Grade 1

a	brothers	fall	heard	more	pull	the	where
about	brown	family	help	most	pushed	their	who
above	buy	far	her	mother	put	there	why
across	by	father	here	my	read	these	window
after	call	few	high	myself	ready	they	with
again	car	field	hold	near	right	think	work
all	carry	find	house	never	said	those	world
almost	caught	first	how	new	school	thought	would
along	city	five	I	night	second	three	write
always	cold	fly	idea	no	see	to	years
and	come	follow	into	noise	seven	today	yellow
animal	could	food	is	nothing	shall	together	you
are	country	for	kinds	now	she	too	young
around	covers	four	know	of	should	took	your
away	cried	friend	large	off	show	toward	
baby	different	friendship	laugh	old	sing	try	**Grade 2**
ball	do	full	learning	once	small	two	air
be	does	funny	light	one	soil	under	cheer
bear	done	give	like	only	some	until	children
beautiful	don't	go	listen	open	sometimes	use	hello
because	door	goes	little	or	soon	very	hundred
been	down	good	live	our	sorry	walk	mind
before	draw	great	long	out	starts	want	next
began	earth	green	look	over	stories	warms	other
begins	eat	ground	loudly	own	story	was	pretty
bird	eight	grow	loved	paper	studied	wash	says
blue	enough	happy	make	party	sure	watch	sleep
both	even	have	many	people	surprised	water	table
boy	every	he	maybe	pictures	take	we	this
bring	everyone	head	me	play	talk	were	told
	eyes	hear	minute	please	teacher	what	

Decoding skills taught to date: short *a*; short *i*; CVC syllable pattern (closed syllables); short *o*; short *u*; short *e*; long *a* (CVC*e*); long *i* (CVC*e*); /k/ spelled *c*; /s/ spelled *c*; long *o* (CVC*e*); long *u* /yōo/ (CVC*e*); long *u* /ōo/ (CVC*e*); long *e* (CVC*e*); /g/ spelled *g*; /j/ spelled *g*, *dge*; blends with *r*; blends with *l*; blends with *s*; final blend *nd*; final blend *ng*; final blend *nk*; final blend *nt*; double final consonants *ll*, *ss*, *ff*, *zz*; consonants *ck*; double consonants (CVC, closed syllables); consonant digraph *th*; consonant digraph *sh*

Swim and Swish

Trish and her dad like to swim at the shore. Waves rush in and out. Trish got a new mask and swim fins. Dad will show Trish how to swim with the swim fins and mask.

1

Dad and Trish swim deep. They see fish and shells.

"This mask helps me see it all!" says Trish. "Thanks, Dad."

4

"Gramps came in, Dad," said Pam.
"Gramps! Dad made you this cake."

"It smells fine! When can we eat it?"
asked Gramps.

"Let me cut it," said Dad, "and then
we can eat."

4

Bake a Cake

Dad had a hot pan in his hands.
"What is that?" asked Pam.
"It is cake," said Dad.
"I like cake!" said Pam.

1

"Get a whiff of that cake!" said Pam.
"It smells fine. When can we eat it?"
Pam asked.

"Not yet," said Dad. "Let it sit for a
while. Then we can frost it with jam."

"That cake is fine," said Pam.
"When can we eat it?"

"We can eat it when Gramps gets in,"
said Dad. "This cake is for him."

"When will Gramps get in?" asked
Pam.

2

3

Watch Chuck Chip

DECODABLE WORDS

Target Skill: consonant digraphs *ch* and *tch*

catch	chin	chop	match
chat	chip	Chuck	much
Chick	chips	fetch	patch

Previously Taught Skills

an	can	has	it	on
and	fast	his	log	this
as	fun	home	logs	until
at	get	if	must	with
back	gets	is	nap	

SKILLS APPLIED IN WORDS IN STORY: short *a*; short *i*; CVC syllable pattern (closed syllables); short *o*; short *u*; short *e*; long *o* (CVCe); /k/ spelled *c*; /g/ spelled *g*; blends with *s*; final blend *nd*; consonants *ck*; consonant digraph *th*; consonant digraphs *ch, tch*
From Grade 1: consonants; short vowels; inflection *-s*

HIGH-FREQUENCY WORDS

a	he	idea	the	watch
comes	how	no	to	work
for	I	says	too	you

© Houghton Mifflin Harcourt Publishing Company

Watch Chuck Chip

High-Frequency Words Taught to Date

Grade 1

a	brothers	fall	hear	more	pull	the	where
about	brown	family	help	most	pushed	their	who
above	buy	far	her	mother	put	there	why
across	by	father	here	my	read	these	window
after	call	few	high	myself	ready	they	with
again	car	field	hold	near	right	think	work
all	carry	find	house	never	said	those	world
almost	caught	first	how	new	school	thought	would
along	city	five	I	night	second	three	write
always	cold	fly	idea	no	see	to	years
and	come	follow	into	noise	seven	today	yellow
animal	could	food	is	nothing	shall	together	you
are	country	for	kinds	now	she	too	young
around	covers	four	know	of	should	took	your
away	cried	friend	large	off	show	toward	
baby	different	friendship	laugh	old	sing	try	**Grade 2**
ball	do	full	learning	once	small	two	air
be	does	funny	light	one	soil	under	cheer
bear	done	give	like	only	some	until	children
beautiful	don't	go	listen	open	sometimes	use	hello
because	door	goes	little	or	soon	very	hundred
been	down	good	live	our	sorry	walk	mind
before	draw	great	long	out	starts	want	next
began	earth	green	look	over	stories	warms	other
begins	eat	ground	loudly	own	story	was	pretty
bird	eight	grow	loved	paper	studied	wash	says
blue	enough	happy	make	party	sure	watch	sleep
both	even	have	many	people	surprised	water	table
boy	every	he	maybe	pictures	take	we	this
bring	everyone	head	me	play	talk	were	told
	eyes	heard	minute	please	teacher	what	

Decoding skills taught to date: short *a;* short *i;* CVC syllable pattern (closed syllables); short *o;* short *u;* short *e;* long *a* (CVC*e*); long *i* (CVC*e*); /k/ spelled *c;* /s/ spelled *c;* long *o* (CVC*e*); long *u* /yōō/ (CVC*e*); long *u* /ōō/ (CVC*e*); long *e* (CVC*e*); /g/ spelled *g;* /j/ spelled *g, dge;* blends with *r;* blends with *l;* blends with *s;* final blend *nd;* final blend *ng;* final blend *nk;* final blend *nt;* double final consonants *ll, ss, ff, zz;* consonants *ck;* double consonants (CVC, closed syllables); consonant digraph *th;* consonant digraph *sh;* consonant digraph *wh;* consonant digraphs *ch, tch*
From Grade 1: consonants; short vowels; inflection *-s*

This log is no match for how fast Chuck can chip. Chuck chips too much. Chuck has to catch a nap. Nap, nap, nap, Chuck.

Watch Chuck Chip

Chuck chips at a log. It is fun to chip logs. Chuck must get the chips to patch his home. Chuck gets chips on his chin. Chip, chip, chip, Chuck.

Steph swims in the pond. Bugs and fish hop and jump. Steph gets them. Phil still looks for phantom bugs and fish that went plop!

4

Phil and Steph

Phil and Steph are ducks. They swim in a nice pond. They dive and splash. They look for fish and bugs to eat.

1

A fish jumps up. Phil and Steph swim fast. Phil gets the fish.

A bug hops. Phil and Steph swim fast. Phil gets the bug.

Steph is mad. Steph has no fish. Steph has no bugs. Phil swims too fast!

Steph gets a rock and hides by a big plant. Phil cannot see Steph.

Will Steph toss the rock? Yes! The rock plops in the pond and makes a splash.

Phil swims fast. No fish and no bugs are here. What made the splash?

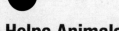

Who Helps Animals?

DECODABLE WORDS

Target Skill: base words and ending -*s* (no spelling changes)

checks	helps	quills
ducks	pets	vets

Previously Taught Skills

and	get	nose	swim	when
back	has	not	take	white
but	help	on	tape	will
can	in	pen	them	with
cat	is	pet	then	
cut	it	ram	these	
dog	its	run	this	
duck	just	sick	vet	
fix	leg	stuck	well	

SKILLS APPLIED IN WORDS IN STORY: short *a*; short *i*; CVC syllable pattern (closed syllables); short *o*; short *u*; short *e*; long *a* (CVC*e*); long *i* (CVC*e*); long *o* (CVC*e*); /k/ spelled *c*; long *e* (CVC*e*); /g/ spelled *g*; blends with *s*; final blend *nd*; double final consonants *ll*; consonants *ck*; consonant digraphs *th*, *sh*, *wh*, *ch*; base words and ending -*s*   **From Grade 1:** consonants; short vowels; final blends; /kw/ spelled *qu*

HIGH-FREQUENCY WORDS

a	don't	she	who
animals	now	the	
both	one	to	
covers	out	walk	

Houghton Mifflin Harcourt

Who Helps Animals?

High-Frequency Words Taught to Date

Grade 1							
a	brown	far	here	myself	right	those	would
about	buy	father	high	near	said	thought	write
above	by	few	hold	never	school	three	years
across	call	field	house	new	second	to	yellow
after	car	find	how	night	see	today	you
again	carry	first	I	no	seven	together	young
all	caught	five	idea	noise	shall	too	your
almost	city	fly	into	nothing	she	took	
along	cold	follow	is	now	should	toward	Grade 2
always	come	food	kinds	of	show	try	air
and	could	for	know	off	sing	two	cheer
animal	country	four	large	old	small	under	children
are	covers	friend	laugh	once	soil	until	hello
around	cried	friendship	learning	one	some	use	hundred
away	different	full	light	only	sometimes	very	mind
baby	do	funny	like	open	soon	walk	next
ball	does	give	listen	or	sorry	want	other
be	done	go	little	our	starts	warms	pretty
bear	don't	goes	live	out	stories	was	says
beautiful	door	good	long	over	story	wash	sleep
because	down	great	look	own	studied	watch	table
been	draw	green	loudly	paper	sure	water	this
before	earth	ground	loved	party	surprised	we	told
began	eat	grow	make	people	take	were	
begins	eight	happy	many	pictures	talk	what	
bird	enough	have	maybe	play	teacher	where	
blue	even	he	me	please	the	who	
both	every	head	minute	pull	their	why	
boy	everyone	hear	more	pushed	there	window	
bring	eyes	heard	most	put	these	with	
brothers	fall	help	mother	read	they	work	
	family	her	my	ready	think	world	

Decoding skills taught to date: short *a*; short *i*; CVC syllable pattern (closed syllables); short *o*; short *u*; short *e*; long *a* (CVC*e*); long *i* (CVC*e*); /k/ spelled *c*; /s/ spelled *c*; long o (CVC*e*); long *u* /yōō/ (CVC*e*); long *u* /ōō/ (CVC*e*); long *e* (CVCe); /g/ spelled *g*; /j/ spelled *g*, *dge*; blends with *r*; blends with *l*; blends with *s*; final blend *nd*; final blend *ng*; final blend *nk*; final blend *nt*; double final consonants *ll*, *ss*, *ff*, *zz*; consonants *ck*; double consonants (CVC, closed syllables); consonant digraph *th*; consonant digraph *sh*; consonant digraph *wh*; consonant digraphs *ch*, *tch*; consonant digraph *ph*; base words and ending -*s* **From Grade 1:** consonants; short vowels; final blends; /kw/ spelled *qu*

The ram is back in its pen. But now the vet has to help a pet dog. It has quills stuck in its nose! The vet will take them out.

Vets like to help animals!

4

Who Helps Animals?

Vets help pets. When a pet is sick, a vet can help it. This vet helps a sick cat. The cat will get well.

1

Sis Yelled

DECODABLE WORDS

Target Skill: base words and ending –*ed* **/d/**

filled	pulled	rolled	yelled

Previously Taught Skills

and	drinks	her	Pat	time
at	fast	his	put	up
back	for	home	ride	us
cart	gave	in	sat	will
cents	get	is	Sis	with
cost	got	it	stand	yell
cup	had	Jon	take	
did	hand	likes	ten	
dime	handed	lot	thanks	
drink	hands	not	then	

SKILLS APPLIED IN WORDS IN STORY: short *a*; short *i*; short *o*; short *u*; short *e*; long *a* (CVC*e*); long *i* (CVC*e*); /k/ spelled *c*; /s/ spelled *c*; long *o* (CVC*e*); /g/ spelled *g*; blends with *r*; blends with *s*; final blend *nd*; final blend *nk*; final blend *nt*; double final consonants *ll*, *ss*, *ff*, *zz*; consonants *ck*; consonant digraph *th*; base words and ending -*s* (no spelling changes); base words and ending -*ed* /ed/ (no spelling changes); base words and ending -*ed* /d/ (no spelling changes) **From Grade 1:** short vowels; consonants; /z/ spelled *s*; *r*-controlled vowels

HIGH-FREQUENCY WORDS

a	happy	said	to	you
do	have	she	want	your
each	I	the	was	
from	now	they	what	

Houghton Mifflin Harcourt

Sis Yelled

High-Frequency Words Taught to Date

Grade 1

a	brothers	fall	heard	more	pull	the	where
about	brown	family	help	most	pushed	their	who
above	buy	far	her	mother	put	there	why
across	by	father	here	my	read	these	window
after	call	few	high	myself	ready	they	with
again	car	field	hold	near	right	think	work
all	carry	find	house	never	said	those	world
almost	caught	first	how	new	school	thought	would
along	city	five	I	night	second	three	write
always	cold	fly	idea	no	see	to	years
and	come	follow	into	noise	seven	today	yellow
animal	could	food	is	nothing	shall	together	you
are	country	for	kinds	now	she	too	young
around	covers	four	know	of	should	took	your
away	cried	friend	large	off	show	toward	
baby	different	friendship	laugh	old	sing	try	**Grade 2**
ball	do	full	learning	once	small	two	air
be	does	funny	light	one	soil	under	cheer
bear	done	give	like	only	some	until	children
beautiful	don't	go	listen	open	sometimes	use	hello
because	door	goes	little	or	soon	very	hundred
been	down	good	live	our	sorry	walk	mind
before	draw	great	long	out	starts	want	next
began	earth	green	look	over	stories	warms	other
begins	eat	ground	loudly	own	story	was	pretty
bird	eight	grow	loved	paper	studied	wash	says
blue	enough	happy	make	party	sure	watch	sleep
both	even	have	many	people	surprised	water	table
boy	every	he	maybe	pictures	take	we	this
bring	everyone	head	me	play	talk	were	told
	eyes	hear	minute	please	teacher	what	

Decoding skills taught to date: short *a*; short *i*; CVC syllable pattern (closed syllables); short *o*; short *u*; short *e*; long *a* (CVC*e*); long *i* (CVC*e*); /k/ spelled *c*; /s/ spelled *c*; long *o* (CVC*e*); long *u* /yo͞o/ (CVC*e*); long *u* /o͞o/ (CVC*e*); long *e* (CVC*e*); /g/ spelled *g*; /j/ spelled *g*, *dge*; blends with *r*; blends with *l*; blends with *s*; final blend *nd*; final blend *ng*; final blend *nk*; final blend *nt*; double final consonants *ll, ss, ff, zz*; consonants *ck*; double consonants (CVC, closed syllables); consonant digraph *th*; consonant digraph *sh*; consonant digraph *wh*; consonant digraphs *ch, tch*; consonant digraph *ph*; base words and ending *-s* (no spelling changes); base words and ending *-ed* /ed/ (no spelling changes); base words and ending *-ed* /d/ (no spelling changes)   **From Grade 1:** short vowels; consonants; /z/ spelled *s*; r-controlled vowels

Then Sis yelled and yelled and yelled. Jon put his hands up.

"Sis likes the drink a lot," Jon said. "Now it is time for us to get home."

Jon pulled and pulled Sis in her cart. The cart rolled and rolled. They got back home fast!

4

Sis Yelled

Sis got in her cart and yelled. She wanted Jon to take her for a ride.

"I will take you for a ride," said Jon. "You do not have to yell!"

Jon pulled and pulled the cart. It rolled and rolled. Sis sat and yelled and yelled.

1

Jon pulled and pulled. Then Sis yelled and yelled.

"What is it?" said Jon.

Sis had her hand up. She wanted to get a drink at the stand. Each cup cost ten cents.

"I will get you a cup," said Jon.

Pat filled a cup with the drink. Jon gave Pat a dime for the drink. Then Jon handed Sis her drink. Sis did not yell. Sis was happy with her drink.

"Thanks," said Jon. "Sis likes the drinks from your stand."

Tom and Duke

DECODABLE WORDS

Target Skill: base words and ending *-ed* /d/

filled   smelled   spilled   yelled

Previously Taught Skills

and	fine	late	pat	Tom
bad	had	like	pile	top
big	he	lot	pot	went
but	him	made	sand	with
can	his	mess	sat	
dog	home	must	spill	
Duke	in	nice	still	
fill	it	on	then	

SKILLS APPLIED IN WORDS IN STORY: short *a*; short *i*; short *o*; short *u*; short *e*; long *a* (CVC*e*); long *i* (CVC*e*); /k/ spelled *c*; /s/ spelled *c*; long *o* (CVC*e*); long *u* /o͞o/ (CVC*e*); /g/ spelled *g*; blends with *s*; final blend *nd*; final blend *nt*; double final consonants *ll*, *ss*, *ff*, *zz*; consonant digraph *th*; base words and ending *-ed* /d/ (no spelling changes) **From Grade 1:** short vowels; consonants; /z/ spelled *s*; long *e* spelled *e*

HIGH-FREQUENCY WORDS

a	good	of	to
again	no	play	too
from	now	the	was

Tom and Duke

Hal Likes Fixing Vans

DECODABLE WORDS

Target Skill: **base words and ending -ing**

adding	fixing	testing	waxing
clicking	picking	ticking	working

Previously Taught Skills

and	gas	makes	shop	vans
at	get	more	so	wire
can	gets	must	stop	with
did	Hal	nice	test	
first	his	no	truck	
fix	is	pick	up	
fixed	likes	picked	van	

SKILLS APPLIED IN WORDS IN STORY: short *a*; short *i*; CVC syllable pattern (closed syllables); short *o*; short *u*; short *e*; CVC syllable pattern (closed syllables); long *a* (CVCe); long *i* (CVCe); /k/ spelled *c*; /s/ spelled *c*; long *o* (CVCe); long *u* /yoō/ (CVCe); long *u* /oō/ (CVCe); long *e* (CVCe); /g/ spelled *g*; /j/ spelled *g*, *dge*; blends with *r*; blends with *l*; blends with *s*; final blend *nd*; final blend *ng*; final blend *nk*; final blend *nt*; double final consonants *ll*, *ss*, *ff*, *zz*; consonants *ck*; double consonants (CVC, closed syllables); consonant digraph *th*; consonant digraph *sh*; consonant digraph *wh*; consonant digraphs *ch*, *tch*; consonant digraph *ph*; base words and endings -*s*, -*ed*; base words and ending -*ing*   **From Grade 1:** consonants, short vowels, final blend *st*; *r*-controlled vowel *ir*, *r*-controlled vowel *ore*

HIGH-FREQUENCY WORDS

a	I	says	to
do	look	the	

Houghton Mifflin Harcourt.

Hal Likes Fixing Vans

High-Frequency Words Taught to Date

Grade 1	brown	far	here	myself	right	those	would
a	buy	father	high	near	said	thought	write
about	by	few	hold	never	school	three	years
above	call	field	house	new	second	to	yellow
across	car	find	how	night	see	today	you
after	carry	first	I	no	seven	together	young
again	caught	five	idea	noise	shall	too	your
all	city	fly	into	nothing	she	took	
almost	cold	follow	is	now	should	toward	*Grade 2*
along	come	food	kinds	of	show	try	air
always	could	for	know	off	sing	two	cheer
and	country	four	large	old	small	under	children
animal	covers	friend	laugh	once	soil	until	hello
are	cried	friendship	learning	one	some	use	hundred
around	different	full	light	only	sometimes	very	mind
away	do	funny	like	open	soon	walk	next
baby	does	give	listen	or	sorry	want	other
ball	done	go	little	our	starts	warms	pretty
be	don't	goes	live	out	stories	was	says
bear	door	good	long	over	story	wash	sleep
beautiful	down	great	look	own	studied	watch	table
because	draw	green	loudly	paper	sure	water	this
been	earth	ground	loved	party	surprised	we	told
before	eat	grow	make	people	take	were	
began	eight	happy	many	pictures	talk	what	
begins	enough	have	maybe	play	teacher	where	
bird	even	he	me	please	the	who	
blue	every	head	minute	pull	their	why	
both	everyone	hear	more	pushed	there	window	
boy	eyes	heard	most	put	these	with	
bring	fall	help	mother	read	they	work	
brothers	family	her	my	ready	think	world	

Decoding skills taught to date: short *a*; short *i*; CVC syllable pattern (closed syllables); short *o*; short *u*; short *e*; CVC syllable pattern (closed syllables); long *a* (CVC*e*); long *i* (CVC*e*); /k/ spelled *c*; /s/ spelled *c*; long *o* (CVC*e*); long *u* /yōō/ (CVC*e*); long *u* /ōō/ (CVC*e*); long *e* (CVC*e*); /g/ spelled *g*; /j/ spelled *g*, *dge*; blends with *r*; blends with *l*; blends with *s*; final blend *nd*; final blend *ng*; final blend *nk*; final blend *nt*; double final consonants *ll, ss, ff, zz*; consonants *ck*; double consonants (CVC, closed syllables); consonant digraph *th*; consonant digraph *sh*; consonant digraph *wh*; consonant digraphs *ch, tch*; consonant digraph *ph*; base words and endings -*s*, -*ed*; base words and ending -*ing*   **From Grade 1:** consonants; short vowels; final blends *st*; r-controlled vowel *ir*; r-controlled vowel *ore*

Waxing makes vans look so nice. Hal can do the waxing! At the van shop Hal is waxing, waxing, waxing. Hal likes waxing vans. Hal can do the picking up, testing, fixing, and waxing. Hal can get vans working!

Hal Likes Fixing Vans

The van must get fixed. Hal can do the fixing! First, Hal must get the van to his shop. The van must get picked up with the pick up truck. Hal gets his truck. Hal can do the picking up!

At the van shop, the van is clicking and ticking, clicking and ticking. "I can fix the clicking and ticking!" says Hal. Hal must test a wire to stop the clicking and ticking. Hal can do the testing!

Hal did the testing. Hal fixed the clicking and ticking. No more clicking and ticking! The van is working! The van must get gas. Hal can get gas. Hal likes adding gas and fixing vans!

Cat Is Missing

DECODABLE WORDS

Target Skill: base words and ending *-ing*

catching	licking	rocking
checking	missing	scratching
jumping	perching	yelling

Previously Taught Skills

bark	for	jump	says	up
can	glad	likes	see	Val
cannot	hide	not	sits	when
Cat	in	perched	stuck	will
catch	is	rocks	that	
did	it	safe	tree	

SKILLS APPLIED IN WORDS IN STORY: short *a*; short *i*; CVC syllable pattern (closed syllables); short *o*; short *u*; short *e*; CVC syllable pattern (closed syllables); long *a* (CVCe); long *i* (CVCe); /k/ spelled *c*; /s/ spelled *c*; long *o* (CVCe); long *u* /yōō/ (CVCe); long *u* /ōō/ (CVCe); long *e* (CVCe); /g/ spelled *g*; /j/ spelled *g*, *dge*; blends with *r*; blends with *l*; blends with *s*; final blend *nd*; final blend *ng*; final blend *nk*; final blend *nt*; double final consonants *ll*, *ss*, *ff*, *zz*; consonants *ck*; double consonants (CVC, closed syllables); consonant digraph *th*; consonant digraph *sh*; consonant digraph *wh*; consonant digraphs *ch*, *tch*; consonant digraph *ph*; base words and endings *-s*, *-ed*; base words and ending *-ing*   **From Grade 1:** consonants, short vowels, final blends *mp*; long *e* (*ee*); blends with *r*; *r*-controlled vowels *ar*, *er*

HIGH-FREQUENCY WORDS

be	I	the	where
find	says	to	you

© Houghton Mifflin Harcourt Publishing Company

Houghton Mifflin Harcourt.

Cat Is Missing

Luke Liked Racing

DECODABLE WORDS

Target Skill: ending *-ing*: drop *e*

biking	hiking	scoring
chasing	racing	skating

Previously Taught Skills

and	got	liked	time
best	grass	Luke	went
fast	hills	on	when
for	in	puck	with
fun	Jeff	score	

SKILLS APPLIED IN WORDS IN STORY: short *a*; short *i*; CVC syllable pattern (closed syllables); short *o*; short *u*; short *e*; CVC syllable pattern (closed syllables); long *a* (CVC*e*); long *i* (CVC*e*); /k/ spelled *c*; /s/ spelled *c*; long *o* (CVC*e*); long *u* /yo͞o/ (CVC*e*); long *u* /o͞o/ (CVC*e*); long *e* (CVC*e*); /g/ spelled *g*; /j/ spelled *g*, *dge*; blends with *r*; blends with *l*; blends with *s*; final blend *nd*; final blend *ng*; final blend *nk*; final blend *nt*; double final consonants *ll*, *ss*, *ff*, *zz*; consonants *ck*; double consonants (CVC, closed syllables); consonant digraph *th*; consonant digraph *sh*; consonant digraph *wh*; consonant digraphs *ch*, *tch*; consonant digraph *ph*; base words and endings *-s*, *-ed*, *-ing*; ending *-ed*: drop *e*; ending *-ing*: drop *e*
From Grade 1: consonants; short vowels; final blend *st*

HIGH-FREQUENCY WORDS

after	he	school	they
all	of	the	

© Houghton Mifflin Harcourt Publishing Company

Houghton Mifflin Harcourt.

Luke Liked Racing

High-Frequency Words Taught to Date

Grade 1

a	brown	far	here	myself	right	those	would
about	buy	father	high	near	said	thought	write
above	by	few	hold	never	school	three	years
across	call	field	house	new	second	to	yellow
after	car	find	how	night	see	today	you
again	carry	first	I	no	seven	together	young
all	caught	five	idea	noise	shall	too	your
almost	city	fly	into	nothing	she	took	
along	cold	follow	is	now	should	toward	**Grade 2**
always	come	food	kinds	of	show	try	afraid
and	could	for	know	off	sing	two	air
animal	country	four	large	old	small	under	cheer
are	covers	friend	laugh	once	soil	until	children
around	cried	friendship	learning	one	some	use	dark
away	different	full	light	only	sometimes	very	few
baby	do	funny	like	open	soon	walk	hello
ball	does	give	listen	or	sorry	want	hundred
be	done	go	little	our	starts	warms	kept
bear	don't	goes	live	out	stories	was	might
beautiful	door	good	long	over	story	wash	mind
because	down	great	look	own	studied	watch	next
been	draw	green	loudly	paper	sure	water	other
before	earth	ground	loved	party	surprised	we	pretty
began	eat	grow	make	people	take	were	says
begins	eight	happy	many	pictures	talk	what	sleep
bird	enough	have	maybe	play	teacher	where	table
blue	even	he	me	please	the	who	this
both	every	head	minute	pull	their	why	told
boy	everyone	hear	more	pushed	there	window	
bring	eyes	heard	most	put	these	with	
brothers	fall	help	mother	read	they	work	
	family	her	my	ready	think	world	

Decoding skills taught to date: short *a*; short *i*; CVC syllable pattern (closed syllables); short *o*; short *u*; short *e*; CVC syllable pattern (closed syllables); long *a* (CVC*e*); long *i* (CVC*e*); /k/ spelled *c*; /s/ spelled *c*; long *o* (CVC*e*); long *u* /yōō/ (CVC*e*); long *u* /ōō/ (CVC*e*); long *e* (CVC*e*); /g/ spelled *g*; /j/ spelled *g, dge*; blends with *r*; blends with *l*; blends with *s*; final blend *nd*; final blend *ng*; final blend *nk*; final blend *nt*; double final consonants *ll, ss, ff, zz*; consonants *ck*; double consonants (CVC, closed syllables); consonant digraph *th*; consonant digraph *sh*; consonant digraph *wh*; consonant digraphs *ch, tch*; consonant digraph *ph*; base words and endings *-s, -ed, -ing*; ending *-ed*: drop *e*; ending *-ing*: drop *e*   **From Grade 1:** consonants; short vowels; final blend *st*

Luke Liked Racing

Luke liked skating. Luke and Jeff went skating for fun. Luke and Jeff liked chasing the puck. Luke got the puck! Score! Luke liked scoring best of all.

Luke liked racing. Luke went racing all the time. Luke liked racing fast. Luke liked racing Jeff. They went racing after school.

© Houghton Mifflin Harcourt Publishing Company

Luke liked biking. He went biking with Jeff. Luke and Jeff liked biking fast. They liked racing when they went biking.

Luke liked hiking. He went hiking with Jeff. They went hiking on hills. They went hiking in grass. They liked hiking.

Baking Day

DECODABLE WORDS

Target Skill: ending -*ing*: drop *e*

baking	making	smiling	tasting

Previously Taught Skills

adds	butter	I	pie	time
am	can	is	places	wait
and	cannot	it	Sam	yes
apple	chops	like	slice	
apples	cuts	likes	slices	
apron	day	make	smell	
asks	hat	Mom	spice	
bake	his	on	start	

SKILLS APPLIED IN WORDS IN STORY: short *a*; short *i*; CVC syllable pattern (closed syllables); short *o*; short *u*; short *e*; CVC syllable pattern (closed syllables); long *a* (CVC*e*); long *i* (CVC*e*); /k/ spelled *c*; /s/ spelled *c*; long *o* (CVC*e*); long *u* /y$\overline{oo}$/ (CVC*e*); long *u* /$\overline{oo}$/ (CVC*e*); long *e* (CVC*e*); /g/ spelled *g*; /j/ spelled *g*, *dge*; blends with *r*; blends with *l*; blends with *s*; final blend *nd*; final blend *ng*; final blend *nk*; final blend *nt*; double final consonants *ll*, *ss*, *ff*, *zz*; consonants *ck*; double consonants (CVC, closed syllables); consonant digraph *th*; consonant digraph *sh*; consonant digraph *wh*; consonant digraphs *ch*, *tch*; consonant digraph *ph*; base words and endings -*s*, -*ed*, -*ing*; ending -*ed*: drop *e*; ending -*ing*: drop *e*
From Grade 1: consonants; short vowels; long *a* spelled *ai* and *ay*; long *i* spelled *i*; *r*-controlled vowel *ar*; long *i* spelling patterns *ie*, *igh*; syllable _*le*

HIGH-FREQUENCY WORDS

a	head	says	today
are	of	the	you
done	ready	to	

Houghton Mifflin Harcourt.

Baking Day

It Isn't Yet

DECODABLE WORDS

Target Skill: **contractions with 's and n't**

can't	isn't	let's
hasn't	it's	that's

Previously Taught Skills

asked	for	look	pick	up
at	get	looked	picked	well
bat	got	make	see	will
be	had	mine	shape	with
box	in	name	tag	yelled
bring	is	nice	tell	yes
can	it	not	think	yet
Dad	kit	on	this	
did	Lon	paper	truck	

SKILLS APPLIED IN WORDS IN STORY: short *a*; short *i*; CVC syllable pattern (closed); CV syllable pattern (open); short *u*; short *e*; long *a* (CVC*e*); long *i* (CVC*e*); /s/ spelled *c*; /g/ spelled *g*; blends with *r*; blends with *s*; final blend *ng*; final blend *nk*; double final consonants *ll*; consonants *ck*; consonant digraph *th*; consonant digraph *sh*; base words and ending –*ed* /d/; base words and ending –*ed* /t/; contractions with 's and *n't*   **From Grade 1:** consonants; short vowels; long *e* (*ee*); vowel digraph *oo* /o͞o/; r-controlled vowels *er*, *or*

HIGH-FREQUENCY WORDS

a	I	the	you
do	said	wanted	
how	saw	what	

It Isn't Yet

High-Frequency Words Taught to Date

Grade 1							Grade 2
a	buy	few	house	night	seven	too	afraid
about	by	field	how	no	shall	took	air
above	call	find	I	noise	she	toward	better
across	car	first	idea	nothing	should	try	cheer
after	carry	five	into	now	show	two	children
again	caught	fly	is	of	sing	under	dark
all	city	follow	kinds	off	small	until	hello
almost	cold	food	know	old	soil	use	hundred
along	come	for	large	once	some	very	kept
always	could	four	laugh	one	sometimes	walk	might
and	country	friend	learning	only	soon	want	mind
animal	covers	friendship	light	open	sorry	warms	next
are	cried	full	like	or	starts	was	other
around	different	funny	listen	our	stories	wash	pretty
away	do	give	little	out	story	watch	really
baby	does	go	live	over	studied	water	says
ball	done	goes	long	own	sure	we	sleep
be	don't	good	look	paper	surprised	were	table
bear	door	great	loudly	party	take	what	this
beautiful	down	green	loved	people	talk	where	
because	draw	ground	make	pictures	teacher	who	
been	earth	grow	many	play	the	why	
before	eat	happy	maybe	please	their	window	
began	eight	have	me	pull	there	with	
begins	enough	he	minute	pushed	these	work	
bird	even	head	more	put	they	world	
blue	every	hear	most	read	think	would	
both	everyone	heard	mother	ready	those	write	
boy	eyes	help	my	right	thought	years	
bring	fall	her	myself	said	three	yellow	
brothers	family	here	near	school	to	you	
brown	far	high	never	second	today	young	
	father	hold	new	see	together	your	

Decoding skills taught to date: short *a*; short *i*; CVC syllable pattern (closed syllables); short *o*; short *u*; short *e*; long *a* (CVC*e*); long *i* (CVC*e*); /k/ spelled *c*; /s/ spelled *c*; long *o* (CVC*e*); long *u* /yo͞o/ (CVC*e*); long *u* /o͞o/ (CVC*e*); long *e* (CVC*e*); /g/ spelled *g*; /j/ spelled *g*, *dge*; blends with *r*; blends with *l*; blends with *s*; final blend *nd*; final blend *ng*; final blend *nk*; final blend *nt*; double final consonants *ll*, *ss*, *ff*, *zz*; consonants *ck*; double consonant (CVC, closed syllables); consonant digraph *th*; consonant digraph *sh*; consonant digraph *wh*; consonant digraphs *ch*, *tch*; consonant digraph *ph*; base words and ending *-s* (no spelling changes); base words and ending *-ed* /ed/ (no spelling changes); base words and ending *-ed* /d/ (no spelling changes); base words and ending *-ed* /t/ (no spelling changes); base words and ending *-ing*; ending *-ed*: drop *e*; ending *-ing*: drop *e*; CV syllable pattern (open syllables); contractions with *'s* and *n't*

"Let's get in the box," said Dad.

"Yes!" yelled Lon. "That's the truck I wanted. It's in this kit! I can make a truck with this kit!"

4

It Isn't Yet

Lon saw Dad bring in a box. It had nice paper on it. Lon did not see a name tag.

Lon looked at the box. "It hasn't got a name tag. Is it mine?" Lon asked.

"Yes, it's for you," said Dad. "Pick it up, Lon."

1

Lon picked up the box.

"It's the truck I wanted!" yelled Lon.

"It isn't a truck," said Dad. "Not yet!"

"How can a truck not be a truck yet?" Lon asked.

"I will not tell yet," said Dad.

"What is in it?" Lon asked.

"Look," said Dad.

"What do you think it is?" asked Dad.

"Well, it isn't a bat!" said Lon. "The box is not a bat shape. I can't see the shape."

Get Rid of Fox

DECODABLE WORDS

Target Skill: contractions with *'s* and *n't*

can't	didn't	he's	it's	that's

Previously Taught Skills

and	did	him	next	time
ask	Dog	his	not	top
asked	Duck	hut	off	up
at	eat	in	on	we
back	for	is	ran	went
bad	Fox	jumped	rest	when
Bat	get	last	rid	why
be	go	licked	sat	will
bit	got	lips	stop	yelled
but	he	lot	thank	
buzzed	Hen	lunch	that	
came	her	my	then	

SKILLS APPLIED IN WORDS IN STORY: short *a*; short *i*; CVC syllable pattern (closed syllables); short *o*; short *u*; short *e*; long *a* (CVC*e*); long *i* (CVC*e*); /g/ spelled *g*; blends with *s*; final blend *mp*; final blend *nd*; final blend *nk*; final blend *nt*; final blend *xt*; double final consonants *ll, ff, zz*; consonants *ck*; consonant digraph *th*; consonant digraph *wh*; consonant digraph *ch*; base words and ending *-s* (no spelling changes); base words and ending *-ed* /d/ (no spelling changes); base words and ending *-ed* /t/ (no spelling changes); contractions with *'s* and *n't* **From Grade 1:** consonants; short vowels; *r*-controlled *er*, *or*; long *e* (*e, ee, ea*); long *i* spelled *y*

HIGH-FREQUENCY WORDS

a	down	of	there
because	friends	said	to
comes	help	see	would
do	I	the	you

Houghton Mifflin Harcourt.

Get Rid of Fox

Pop! Pop! Pop!

DECODABLE WORDS

Target Skill: **contractions with 've and 're**

we're	we've	you're	you've

Previously Taught Skills

and	check	Jen	not	then
bang	drop	jumped	off	this
be	get	let's	pop	us
Ben	going	lid	popping	waiting
big	got	lots	pot	we
bit	hot	made	Red	will
but	in	make	snack	yelled
came	is	mop	stop	yet
can	it	much	Ted	yum

SKILLS APPLIED IN WORDS IN STORY: short *a*; short *i*; CVC syllable pattern (closed); short *o*; short *u*; short *e*; long *a* (CVC*e*); /g/ spelled *g*; blends with *r*; blends with *s*; final blend *nd*; final blend *ng*; final blend *mp*; double final consonants *ll, ff*; consonants *ck*; consonant digraph *th*; consonant digraph *ch*; base words and ending -*s* (no spelling changes); base words and ending -*ed* /d/ (no spelling changes); base words and ending -*ed* /ed/ (no spelling changes); base words and ending -*ed* /t/ (no spelling changes); base words and ending -*ing* (no spelling changes); contractions with '*s*; contractions with '*ve* and '*re*   **From Grade 1:** consonants; short vowels; long *a* spelled *ai*; base words and ending -*ing* (double final consonant before ending)

HIGH-FREQUENCY WORDS

a	friend(s)	more	the
come	have	of	to
eat	help	put	too
for	I	said	were

Houghton Mifflin Harcourt.

Pop! Pop! Pop!

High-Frequency Words Taught to Date

Grade 1	brown	far	here	myself	right	those	would
a	buy	father	high	near	said	thought	write
about	by	few	hold	never	school	three	years
above	call	field	house	new	second	to	yellow
across	car	find	how	night	see	today	you
after	carry	first	I	no	seven	together	young
again	caught	five	idea	noise	shall	too	your
all	city	fly	into	nothing	she	took	
almost	cold	follow	is	now	should	toward	Grade 2
along	come	food	kinds	of	show	try	afraid
always	could	for	know	off	sing	two	air
and	country	four	large	old	small	under	better
animal	covers	friend	laugh	once	soil	until	cheer
are	cried	friendship	learning	one	some	use	children
around	different	full	light	only	sometimes	very	dark
away	do	funny	like	open	soon	walk	hello
baby	does	give	listen	or	sorry	want	hundred
ball	done	go	little	our	starts	warms	kept
be	don't	goes	live	out	stories	was	might
bear	door	good	long	over	story	wash	mind
beautiful	down	great	look	own	studied	watch	next
because	draw	green	loudly	paper	sure	water	other
been	earth	ground	loved	party	surprised	we	pretty
before	eat	grow	make	people	take	were	really
began	eight	happy	many	pictures	talk	what	says
begins	enough	have	maybe	play	teacher	where	sleep
bird	even	he	me	please	the	who	table
blue	every	head	minute	pull	their	why	this
both	everyone	hear	more	pushed	there	window	told
boy	eyes	heard	most	put	these	with	
bring	fall	help	mother	read	they	work	
brothers	family	her	my	ready	think	world	

Decoding skills taught to date: short *a*; short *i*; CVC syllable pattern (closed); short *o*; short *u*; short *e*; long *a* (CVC*e*); long *i* (CVC*e*); /k/ spelled *c*; /s/ spelled *c*; long *o* (CVC*e*); long *u* /yoo/ (CVC*e*); long *u* /oo/ (CVC*e*); long *e* (CVC*e*); /g/ spelled *g*; /j/ spelled *g, dge*; blends with *r*; blends with *l*; blends with *s*; final blend *nd*; final blend *ng*; final blend *nk*; final blend *nt*; double final consonants *ll, ss, ff, zz*; consonants *ck*; double consonant (CVC, closed syllables); consonant digraph *th*; consonant digraph *sh*; consonant digraph *wh*; consonant digraphs *ch, tch*; consonant digraph *ph*; base words and ending -*s* (no spelling changes); base words and ending -*ed* /ed/ (no spelling changes); base words and ending -*ed* /d/ (no spelling changes); base words and ending -*ed* /t/ (no spelling changes); base words and ending -*ing* (no spelling changes); ending -*ed*: drop *e*; ending -*ing*: drop *e*; CV syllable pattern (open syllables); contractions with '*s* and *n't*; contractions with '*ll* and '*d*; contractions with '*ve* and '*re*

Pop! Pop! Pop!

"Come in, Ben," said Red, Jen, and Ted. "We've made a big snack. It is too much for us. You're going to help us eat it."

"Yum! Yum!" said Ben.

Jen, Red, and Ted were friends.

"Let's make a snack," said Jen. "We've got a pot."

Jen got the pot. "It will be hot in a bit. Then it will pop, and we can eat this snack."

4

1

Ted came in to check the pot.

"We're waiting for a snack, but the pot is not hot yet. I will drop more of this in," said Ted. "Then we will have lots of popping and a big snack."

Pop! Pop! Pop! Pop! Bang! Bang! Bang! The pot lid jumped off.

"You've put too much in the pot!" yelled Red. "It will not stop!"

"Get the pot!" yelled Red.

"Get a mop!" yelled Ted.

"Get help!" yelled Jen.

What Is It?

DECODABLE WORDS

Target Skill: **contractions with** *'ve* **and** *'re*

we're	we've	you're	you've

Previously Taught Skills

an	cat	it's	see	up
and	cute	last	seen	wait
asked	did	leg	shake	waited
at	going	made	shaking	well
big	got	makes	smiled	will
branch	happened	Mel	tail	yelled
but	in	much	that	
Cam	is	must	then	
came	isn't	not	think	
can't	it	pal	tree	

SKILLS APPLIED IN WORDS IN STORY: short *a*; short *i*; CVC syllable pattern (closed); short *o*; short *u*; short *e*; long *a* (CVC*e*); /k/ spelled *c*; long *u* /yoo/ (CVC*e*); /g/ spelled *g*; blends with *r*; blends with *s*; final blend *nd*; final blend *nk*; double final consonants *ll*; double consonant (CVC, closed syllables); consonant digraph *th*; consonant digraph *sh*; consonant digraph *ch*; base words and ending -*s* (no spelling changes); base words and ending -*ed* /ed/ (no spelling changes); base words and ending -*ed* /d/ (no spelling changes); base words and ending -*ed* /ed/ (no spelling changes); base words and ending -*ed* /t/ (no spelling changes); ending -*ing*; drop *e*; contractions with *'s* and *n't*; contractions with *'ve* and *'re*   **From Grade 1:** consonants; short vowels; long *a* spelled *ai*; long *e* spelled *ee*

HIGH-FREQUENCY WORDS

a	down	said	to	what
animal	I	small	was	
be	look(ed)	the	we	

Houghton Mifflin Harcourt

What Is It?

High-Frequency Words Taught to Date

Grade 1							Grade 2
a	buy	few	house	night	seven	too	afraid
about	by	field	how	no	shall	took	air
above	call	find	I	noise	she	toward	better
across	car	first	idea	nothing	should	try	cheer
after	carry	five	into	now	show	two	children
again	caught	fly	is	of	sing	under	dark
all	city	follow	kinds	off	small	until	hello
almost	cold	food	know	old	soil	use	hundred
along	come	for	large	once	some	very	kept
always	could	four	laugh	one	sometimes	walk	might
and	country	friend	learning	only	soon	want	mind
animal	covers	friendship	light	open	sorry	warms	next
are	cried	full	like	or	starts	was	other
around	different	funny	listen	our	stories	wash	pretty
away	do	give	little	out	story	watch	really
baby	does	go	live	over	studied	water	says
ball	done	goes	long	own	sure	we	sleep
be	don't	good	look	paper	surprised	were	table
bear	door	great	loudly	party	take	what	this
beautiful	down	green	loved	people	talk	where	told
because	draw	ground	make	pictures	teacher	who	
been	earth	grow	many	play	the	why	
before	eat	happy	maybe	please	their	window	
began	eight	have	me	pull	there	with	
begins	enough	he	minute	pushed	these	work	
bird	even	head	more	put	they	world	
blue	every	hear	most	read	think	would	
both	everyone	heard	mother	ready	those	write	
boy	eyes	help	my	right	thought	years	
bring	fall	her	myself	said	three	yellow	
brothers	family	here	near	school	to	you	
brown	far	high	never	second	today	young	
	father	hold	new	see	together	your	

Decoding skills taught to date: short *a*; short *i*; CVC syllable pattern (closed); short *o*; short *u*; short *e*; long *a* (CVC*e*); long *i* (CVC*e*); /k/ spelled *c*; /s/ spelled *c*; long *o* (CVC*e*); long *u* /yoo/ (CVC*e*); long *u* /oo/ (CVC*e*); long *e* (CVC*e*), /g/ spelled *g*; /j/ spelled *g*, *dge*; blends with *r*; blends with *l*; blends with *s*; final blend *nd*; final blend *ng*; final blend *nk*; final blend *nt*; double final consonants *ll*, *ss*, *ff*, *zz*; consonants *ck*; double consonant (CVC, closed syllables); consonant digraph *th*; consonant digraph *sh*; consonant digraph *wh*; consonant digraphs *ch*, *tch*; consonant digraph *ph*; base words and ending -*s* (no spelling changes); base words and ending -*ed* /ed/ (no spelling changes); base words and ending -*ed* /d/ (no spelling changes); base words and ending -*ed* /ed/ (no spelling changes); base words and ending -*ed* /t/ (no spelling changes); base words and ending -*ing* (no spelling changes); ending -*ed*: drop *e*; ending -*ing*: drop *e*; CV syllable pattern (open syllables); contractions with *'s* and *n't*; contractions with *'ll* and *'d*; contractions with *'ve* and *'re*

5. Suppose $y = f(x)$ and $\frac{dy}{dx} = x - \frac{y}{2}$. If $f(1) = 2$, then $\lim\limits_{x \to 1} \frac{f(x) - 2}{(x-1)^2} =$

(A) -1 (B) $-\frac{1}{2}$ (C) 0   (D) $\frac{1}{2}$ (E) 1

6. The volume of the parallelepiped which has edges parallel to and the same lengths as the position vectors $\mathbf{u} = \langle 0, 2, 0 \rangle$, $\mathbf{v} = \langle 1, -1, 0 \rangle$, and $\mathbf{w} = \langle -2, 2, 1 \rangle$ is

(A) $\frac{1}{2}$ (B) $\frac{3}{4}$ (C) 2   (D) 15   (E) $13\sqrt{6}$

7. Consider the system

$$\begin{cases} y = 2 \\ y = a(x-b)^2 + c, \end{cases}$$

where a, b, and c are real numbers. For which of the following values of a, b, and c is there a solution to the system of equations?

(A) $a = -9$, $b = -4$, and $c = -5$

(B) $a = 7$, $b = -10$, and $c = 6$

(C) $a = 1$, $b = -6$, and $c = -4$

(D) $a = 2$, $b = 9$, and $c = 4$

(E) $a = -10$, $b = -10$, and $c = -6$

[handwritten:] $2 = (-9)(x+4)^2 - 5 = -9(x^2+8x+16)-5 = -9x^2-72x$

$2 = (7)(x+10)^2 + 6$

$2 = (x+6)^2 - 4 \qquad x^2 + 12x + 32 = 2$

$2 = 2(x-9)^2 + 4 = 2(x^2-18x+81)+4 = 2x^2-36x+166=2$
$\qquad\qquad x^2-18x+83$

$2 = -10(x+10)^2 - 6 \qquad 8 = -10(x+10)^2$

$\frac{8!}{162}$

8. The lateral surface area of a cone is 6π and its slant height is 6. What is the radius of the cone's base?

(A) $\frac{1}{2}$ (B) 1   (C) $\frac{3}{2}$ (D) 2   (E) $\frac{12}{\pi}$

9. What is the measure of the angle between $\mathbf{u} = \langle 2, 0, 2 \rangle$ and $\mathbf{v} = \langle 3\sqrt{2}, -6\sqrt{3}, 3\sqrt{2} \rangle$ in xyz-space?

(A) $0°$ (B) $30°$ (C) $45°$ (D) $60°$ (E) $90°$

10. If U and V are 3-dimensional subspaces of $\mathbb{R}^5$, what are the possible dimensions of $U \cap V$?

(A) 0   (B) 1   (C) 0 or 1   (D) 1, 2, or 3   (E) 0, 1, 2, or 3

[handwritten:] $3+3 - U\cap V \le 5$
$6 - U\cap V \le 5$
$U\cap V \ge 1$

11. What is the absolute minimum value of $f(x) = \frac{x^2 - 6x}{1 + |x + 1|}$?

(A) -2 (B) -1 (C) 0   (D) $\frac{1}{4}$ (E) 7

[handwritten:] $f'(x) = (1+|x+1|)(2x-6) - (x^2-6x)$

12. Suppose T is a linear transformation from $\mathbb{R}^2$ to $\mathbb{R}$ such that $T\begin{pmatrix} 1 \\ -3 \end{pmatrix} = 5$ and $T\begin{pmatrix} 1 \\ 1 \end{pmatrix} = -2$. Then

$T\begin{pmatrix} 0 \\ 2 \end{pmatrix} =$

(A) -4

(B) $-\dfrac{7}{2}$

(C) -1

(D) 3

(E) $\dfrac{9}{2}$

Handwritten work:

$x - 3y = 5$
$-(x + y = -2)$
$\underline{}$
$-4y = 7$
$y = -\dfrac{7}{4}$

$x + y = -2$
$x - \dfrac{7}{4} = -2$
$x - \dfrac{7}{4} = -\dfrac{8}{4}$
$x = -\dfrac{1}{4}$

$-\dfrac{1}{4}(0) - \dfrac{7}{4}(2) = -\dfrac{14}{4} = -\dfrac{7}{2}$

13. If $f(x) = (1-x)^{17}e^{2x}$, then $f^{(17)}(1) =$

(A) $-(17!2^{17}e^2)$

(B) $-(17!e^2)$

(C) 0

(D) $17!2^{17}e^2$

(E) $17!e^2$

Handwritten work:

$f(x) = (1-x)^{17}e^{2x}$

$f'(x) = -17(1-x)^{16}e^{2x} + 2e^{2x}(1-x)^{17} = -17e^{2x}(1-x)^{16} + 2e^{2x}(1-x)^{17}$

$e^{2x}(-17$

$f''(x) = -34e^{2x}(1-x)^{16} + 17e^{2x}16(1-x)^{15} + 4e^{2x}(1-x)^{17}$

14. A large class is to be divided into teams and each student must be a member of exactly one team. However, each student dislikes three of their classmates. Dislike between students need not be mutual. If the teams do <u>not</u> need to be equally sized, how many must be created so that no student is the teammate of someone they dislike?

(A) 4

(B) 7

(C) 10

(D) 13

(E) 16

15. Which of the following could be the graph of a solution of $\dfrac{dy}{dx} = x\,|y|$?

(A)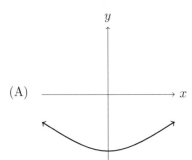

(B)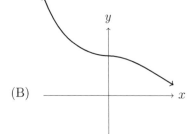

(C)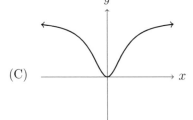

(D)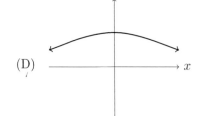

(E)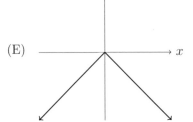

16. Suppose $n\mathbb{Z} = \{0, n, -n, 2n, -2n, \ldots\}$ and $I_n = n\mathbb{Z} \cap [1, 1000]$. How many elements are contained in the set $I_6 \cup I_{15} \cup I_{25}$?

$6\mathbb{Z} = 0, 6, -6, 12, -12, \cdots$

(A) 200   (B) 226   (C) 257   (D) 266   (E) 272

17. If $S = [0, 1] \times [1, 3]$, then $\displaystyle\iint_S xy^2 \, dA =$

(A) $\dfrac{1}{6}$ (B) $\dfrac{1}{3}$ (C) 1   (D) $\dfrac{9}{2}$ (E) $\dfrac{13}{3}$

5

GO ON TO THE NEXT PAGE.

18. Suppose $\mathcal{F}$ is the set of functions such that $f(x) = \dfrac{ax + b}{cx + d}$, where the coefficients a, b, c, and d are real numbers and $ad - bc = 1$. Which of the following are TRUE?

   I. If f and g are in $\mathcal{F}$, then $f \circ g = g \circ f$.

   II. There is a function i in $\mathcal{F}$ such that $i \circ f = f \circ i$ for all f in $\mathcal{F}$.

   III. If f, g, and h are in $\mathcal{F}$, then $f \circ (g \circ h) = (f \circ g) \circ h$.

(A) I only

(B) II only

(C) I and II only

(D) II and III only

(E) I, II, and III

---

19. The region contained between the Lemniscate curve

$$r^2 = 4 \sin 2\theta$$

and the circle $r = \sqrt{2}$ has area

(A) $\sqrt{3} - \dfrac{\pi}{3}$

(B) $2\sqrt{3} - \dfrac{2\pi}{3}$

(C) $2\sqrt{3} - \dfrac{\pi\sqrt{2}}{3}$

(D) $2\sqrt{3} - \dfrac{\pi}{3}$

(E) $2 - \dfrac{\pi}{3}$

GO ON TO THE NEXT PAGE.

20. Let f be a differentiable real-valued function such that $f(3) = 7$ and $f'(x) \geq x$ for all positive x. What is the maximum possible value of $\int_0^3 f(x)\,dx$?

(A) 0

(B) $\dfrac{9}{2}$

(C) 12

(D) $\dfrac{25}{2}$

(E) 21

21. If $f : (0,1) \to (0,1]$, then which of the following could be TRUE?

I. f is one-to-one and onto.

II. The image of f is compact.

III. f is continuous, one-to-one, and onto.

(A) I only

(B) II only

(C) I and II only

(D) I and III only

(E) I, II, and III

22. Suppose
$$f(x) = \begin{cases} \dfrac{2|x|}{5}, & \text{if } -1 \leq x < 2 \\ 0, & \text{otherwise.} \end{cases}$$

Then $\displaystyle\int_{-\infty}^{\infty} x f(x)\,dx =$

(A) $\dfrac{14}{15}$ (B) 1 (C) $\dfrac{6}{5}$ (D) $\dfrac{7}{3}$ (E) 3

23. For which value of n are there exactly two abelian groups of order n up to isomorphism?

(A) 4 (B) 7 (C) 8 (D) 24 (E) none of these

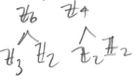

7

GO ON TO THE NEXT PAGE.

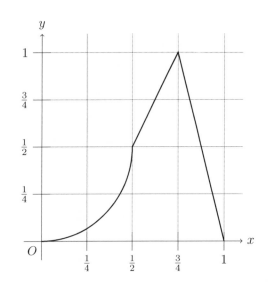

---

24. Above is the graph of $y = f(x)$. If $f(1+x) = f(x)$ for all real x, then $f'(25\pi) =$

(A) -16

(B) 0

(C) undefined

(D) 2

(E) not uniquely determined by the information given

---

25. The convergent sequence $\{x_n\}$ is defined by the recursive relationship $x_1 = 1$ and $x_{n+1} = \sqrt{15 - 2x_n}$ for all positive integers n. What is the value of $\lim_{n \to \infty} x_n$?

(A) -5 (B) -3 (C) 0 (D) 3 (E) 5

GO ON TO THE NEXT PAGE.

x	$f(x)$	$f'(x)$	$g(x)$
-6	-5	1	-3
-2	$-\dfrac{5}{2}$	$\dfrac{1}{4}$	0
2	0	1	6
6	2	3	$\dfrac{13}{2}$

26. If f and g in the table above are inverses, then $(g' \circ g)(0) =$

(A) -1 (B) $-\dfrac{1}{2}$ (C) $\dfrac{1}{3}$ (D) 1 (E) 4

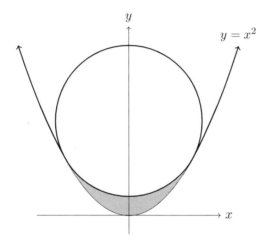

27. A circle of radius 1 is tangent to $y = x^2$ at two points. What is the area of the region bounded by the parabola and circle?

(A) $\dfrac{2}{3} - \dfrac{\pi}{6}$ (B) $\sqrt{3} - \dfrac{11\pi}{24}$ (C) $\dfrac{3\sqrt{3}}{4} - \dfrac{\pi}{3}$ (D) $\dfrac{2}{3} - \dfrac{\pi}{12}$ (E) $\dfrac{11}{6} - \dfrac{\pi}{6}$

28. The arc length of the curve C from the point $(8, 1)$ to the point $(8e, e^2 - 8)$, where

$$C = \{(x, y) \in \mathbb{R}^2 : x = 8e^{t/2} \text{ and } y = e^t - 4t\} ,$$

is which of the following?

(A) $7 - e^2$ (B) $7 - e$ (C) $e^2 - 7$ (D) $e + 7$ (E) $e^2 + 7$

GO ON TO THE NEXT PAGE.

29. Consider a segment of length 10. Points A and B are chosen randomly such that A and B divide the segment into three smaller segments. What is the probability that the three smaller segments could form the sides of a triangle?

(A) 10%   (B) 12.5%   (C) 25%   (D) 37.5%   (E) 50%

30. A discrete graph is complete if there is an edge connecting any pair of vertices. How many edges does a complete graph with 10 vertices have?

(A) 10   (B) 20   (C) 25   (D) 45   (E) 90

31. Suppose P is the set of polynomials with coefficients in $\mathbb{Z}_5$ and degree less than or equal to 7. If the operator D sends $p(x)$ in P to its derivative $p'(x)$, what are the dimensions of the null space n and range r of D ?

(A) $n = 1$ and $r = 6$

(B) $n = 1$ and $r = 7$

(C) $n = 2$ and $r = 5$

(D) $n = 2$ and $r = 6$

(E) $n = 3$ and $r = 5$

32. Consider the following algorithm, which takes two positive input integers a and b and prints a positive output integer.

```
input(a)
input(b)
   begin
      if a > b
         set max = a
         set min = b
      else
         set max = b
         set min = a
      while min > 0
         begin
            set r = max mod min
            replace max = min
            replace min = r
         end
      print a*b/max
   end
```

If a = 20 and b = 28 are the inputs of the following algorithm, what is the result?

(A) 4   (B) 5   (C) 7   (D) 140   (E) 560

10

33. Let $\varphi(k)$ be a proposition which is either true or false depending on the integer k. Suppose that if $\varphi(k)$ is false then so is $\varphi(k-1)$. If there is some k_0 such that $\varphi(k_0)$ is true, what is the strongest conclusion that can be drawn?

(A) $\varphi(k)$ is true for all k.

(B) $\varphi(k_0+1)$ is true.

(C) $\varphi(k_0-1)$ is ture.

(D) $\varphi(k)$ is true for $k \leq k_0$.

(E) $\varphi(k)$ is true for $k \geq k_0$.

34. Define
$$f(x) = \begin{cases} \sin \dfrac{1}{x}, & \text{if } x \neq 0 \\ 0, & \text{if } x = 0. \end{cases}$$

Let $I = \left\{ (x, f(x)) \in \mathbb{R}^2 : -1 \leq x \leq 1 \right\}$. Which of the following are TRUE?

I. The set I is connected.

II. The set I is path connected.

III. The set I is compact.

(A) I only

(B) III only

(C) I and II only

(D) I and III only

(E) I, II, and III

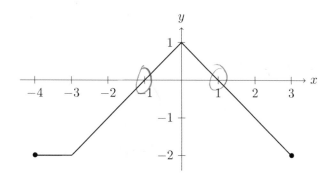

35. The figure above shows the graph of the function f. Suppose that $g(x) = \displaystyle\int_0^x f(t)\, dt$. The absolute maximum of g is

(A) $g(-4)$ (B) $g(-3)$ (C) $g(-1)$ (D) $g(1)$ (E) $g(3)$

11

36. Let $f(x) = \int_0^{x^2} \sqrt{t} \sin \frac{1}{t} \, dt$, and let $I = [-1,0) \cup (0,1]$. Which of the following are TRUE?

   I. f is bounded on the set I.

   II. f' is bounded on the set I.

   III. f'' is bounded on the set I.

(A) I only

(B) II only

(C) I and II only

(D) I and III only

(E) I, II, and III

37. Suppose

$$A = \begin{pmatrix} 1 & 0 & -2 \\ c & -9 & -c \\ 0 & c & -1 \end{pmatrix} .$$

For what value(s) of c is A singular?

(A) -3 (B) -2 (C) -3 and 2 (D) -2 and 2 (E) -3 and 3

38. The region in the first quadrant bounded by the x-axis and the function

$$f(x) = \frac{x}{1 + x^3}$$

is rotated about the x-axis. What is the volume of the solid generated?

(A) $\frac{\pi}{3}$ (B) $\frac{\pi}{4}$ (C) π (D) 2π (E) ∞

$V = \int_0^\cdot \pi \left(top - bottom \right) \, dx$

GO ON TO THE NEXT PAGE.

39. Suppose

for all $\varepsilon > 0$ there exists a $\delta > 0$ such that for all x and y in D

$$|x - y| < \delta \quad \text{implies} \quad |f(x) - f(y)| < \varepsilon .$$

Consider the following statements.

A: For all $\varepsilon > 0$ there is a $\delta > 0$

B: For all x and y in D

C: $|x - y| < \delta$

D: $|f(x) - f(y)| \geq \varepsilon$

Using the letters listed above, the proposition originally stated is which of the following? Denote "not" by $\neg$.

(A) $A\Big(B(C \text{ or } D)\Big)$

(B) $A\Big(B(\neg C \text{ and } D)\Big)$

(C) $\neg A\Big(B(\neg C \text{ or } D)\Big)$

(D) $A\Big(\neg B(\neg C \text{ or } D)\Big)$

(E) $A\Big(B(\neg C \text{ or } \neg D)\Big)$

40. The radius of convergence of the series $\displaystyle\sum_{n=1}^{\infty} \frac{(nx)^n}{2 \cdot 4 \cdot 6 \cdot \ldots \cdot 2n}$ is

(A) 0   (B) $\dfrac{2}{e^2}$ (C) $\dfrac{2}{e}$ (D) $\dfrac{e}{2}$ (E) ∞

13

GO ON TO THE NEXT PAGE.

41. Suppose V is a real vector space of finite dimension n. Call the set of matrices from V into itself $\mathcal{M}(V)$. Let T be in $\mathcal{M}(V)$. Consider the two subspaces

$$\mathcal{U} = \{X \in \mathcal{M}(V) : TX = XT\} \quad \text{and} \quad \mathcal{W} = \{TX - XT : X \in \mathcal{M}(V)\}.$$

Which of the following must be TRUE?

   I. If V has a basis containing only eigenvectors of T then $\mathcal{U} = \mathcal{M}(V)$.

   II. $\dim(\mathcal{U}) + \dim(\mathcal{W}) = n^2$

   III. $\dim(\mathcal{W}) > n$

(A) I only

(B) II only

(C) III only

(D) I and II only

(E) I, II, and III

---

42. If the finite group G contains a subgroup of order five but no element of G other than the identity is its own inverse, then the order of G could be

(A) 8   (B) 20   (C) 30   (D) 35   (E) 42

---

43. If $\zeta = e^{\frac{2\pi}{5}i}$, then $3 + 3\zeta + 12\zeta^2 + 12\zeta^3 + 12\zeta^4 + 9\zeta^5 + 5\zeta^6 =$

(A) $-4e^{\frac{2\pi i}{5}}$ (B) $-4e^{\frac{4\pi i}{5}}$ (C) 0   (D) $4e^{\frac{2\pi i}{5}}$ (E) $4e^{\frac{4\pi i}{5}}$

---

44. Suppose A is a 3×3 matrix such that

$$\det(A - \lambda I) = -\lambda^3 + 3\lambda^2 + \lambda - 3,$$

where I is the 3×3 identity matrix. Which of the following are TRUE of A?

   I. The trace of A is 3.

   II. The determinate of A is -3.

   III. The matrix A has eigenvalues -3 and 1.

(A) I only

(B) II only

(C) III only

(D) I and II only

(E) I, II, and III

GO ON TO THE NEXT PAGE.

45. What is the general solution of

$$2\frac{d^2y}{dx^2} + 9\frac{dy}{dx} - 35y = 0 ?$$

(A) $y = C_1 e^{-7x} + C_2 e^{\frac{5}{2}x}$

(B) $y = C_1 e^{-\frac{5}{2}x} + C_2 e^{7x}$

(C) $y = C_1 e^{-7x} + C_2 e^{5x}$

(D) $y = C_1 e^{-5x} + C_2 e^{7x}$

(E) $y = C_1 \cos(5x) + C_2 \cos(7x)$

46. Let $f(x, y) = x^3 - y^3 + 3x^2y - x$ for all real x and y . Which of the following is TRUE of f ?

(A) There is an absolute minimum at $\left(\frac{1}{3}, \frac{1}{3}\right)$.

(B) There is a relative maximum at $\left(-\frac{1}{3}, -\frac{1}{3}\right)$.

(C) There is a saddle point at $\left(\frac{\sqrt{3}}{3}, -\frac{\sqrt{3}}{3}\right)$.

(D) There is an absolute maximum at $\left(-\frac{\sqrt{3}}{3}, \frac{\sqrt{3}}{3}\right)$.

(E) All critical values are on the line $y = x$.

47. The difference $\log(1.1) - p(1.1)$, where

$$p(x) = x - 1 - \frac{1}{2}(x-1)^2 \ ,$$

is approximately

(A) $-\dfrac{1}{3} \times 10^{-3}$

(B) $-\dfrac{1}{4} \times 10^{-4}$

(C) $\dfrac{3}{8} \times 10^{-5}$

(D) $\dfrac{1}{4} \times 10^{-4}$

(E) $\dfrac{1}{3} \times 10^{-3}$

48. Suppose today is Wednesday. What day of the week will it be $10^{10^{10}}$ days from now?

(A) Sunday

(B) Monday

(C) Tuesday

(D) Wednesday

(E) Thursday

49. It takes Kate k days to write a GRE math practice test. It takes John j days to write a GRE math practice test. If Kate and John work on a practice test in alternating 2-day shifts, it takes them 10 days when Kate starts and 10.5 days when John starts. How long would it take the two to complete a practice test if Kate and John worked simultaneously?

(A) $\dfrac{9}{2}$ days   (B) 5 days   (C) $\dfrac{41}{8}$ days   (D) $\dfrac{36}{7}$ days   (E) 6 days

50. In the complex plane, let C be the circle $|z + 2| = 3$ with positive (counterclockwise) orientation. Then

$$\int_C \frac{dz}{z^3(z-2)} =$$

(A) $-\dfrac{\pi i}{4}$ (B) 0   (C) $\dfrac{3\pi i}{8}$ (D) $\dfrac{7\pi i}{8}$ (E) $2\pi i$

GO ON TO THE NEXT PAGE.

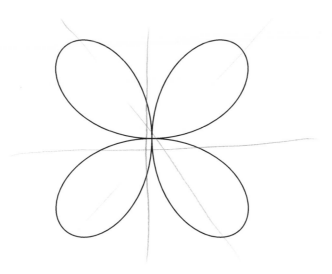

51. A four-petaled rose curve has a group of symmetries which is isomorphic to the

(A) symmetric group S_4

(B) alternating group A_5

(C) cyclic group of order 4

(D) cyclic group of order 8

(E) dihedral group of 8 elements

52. Suppose the real-valued function f has a continuous derivative for all values of x in $\mathbb{R}$. Which of the following must be FALSE?

I. For some closed interval $[a, b]$ and every natural number N there exists an x in the interval $[a, b]$ such that $|f(x)| > N$.

II. For each real number c there are exactly two solutions of $f(x) = c$.

III. The limit $\lim_{x \to \infty} \dfrac{f(x)}{x} = \infty$ if and only if $\lim_{x \to \infty} f'(x) = \infty$.

(A) I only

(B) II only

(C) III only

(D) I and II only

(E) I, II, and III

53. Water drips out of a hole at the vertex of an upside down cone at a rate of 3 cm^3 per minute. The cone's height and radius are 2 cm and 1 cm, respectively. At what rate does the height of the water change when the water level is half a centimeter below the top of the cone? The volume of a cone is $V = \frac{\pi}{3}r^2 h$, where r is the radius and h is the height of the cone.

(A) $-\dfrac{48}{\pi}$ cm/min   (B) $-\dfrac{4}{3\pi}$ cm/min   (C) $-\dfrac{8}{3\pi}$ cm/min   (D) $-\dfrac{24}{\pi}$ cm/min   (E) $-\dfrac{16}{3\pi}$ cm/min

GO ON TO THE NEXT PAGE.

54. Suppose f is an analytic function of the complex variable $z = x + iy$ where x and y are real variables. If

$$f(z) = g(x,y) + e^y i \sin x$$

and $g(x,y)$ is a real-valued function of x and y, what is the value of

$$g\left(\frac{\pi}{2}, 7\right) - g(0,0) \ ?$$

(A) $1 + e^7$

(B) $1 - e^7$

(C) 1

(D) $e^7 - 1$

(E) $2 - 2e^7$

---

55. Suppose A and B are $n \times n$ matrices with real entries. Which of the follow are TRUE?

   I. The trace of A^2 is nonnegative.

   II. If $A^2 = A$, then the trace of A is nonnegative.

   III. The trace of AB is the product of the traces of A and B .

(A) II only

(B) III only

(C) I and II only

(D) II and III only

(E) I, II, and III

---

56. Consider the independent random variables X_i such that either $X_i = 0$ or $X_i = 1$ and each event is equally as likely. Let

$$X = X_1 + X_2 + \ldots + X_{100} \ .$$

Which of the following values is largest?

(A) $\mathrm{Var}(X)$

(B) $100P\left(|X - 50| > 25\right)$

(C) $\displaystyle\sum_{k=0}^{100} k \binom{100}{k} \left(\frac{1}{2}\right)^k$

(D) $100P\left(X \geq 60\right)$

(E) 30

---

57. $\displaystyle\lim_{n \to \infty} \frac{1}{n} + \frac{1}{2+n} + \frac{1}{4+n} + \ldots + \frac{1}{3n} =$

(A) $\dfrac{1}{2}\log 2$ (B) $\dfrac{3}{4}$ (C) $\log\sqrt{3}$ (D) 1 (E) 2

GO ON TO THE NEXT PAGE.

58. Suppose A and A_k are subsets of $\mathbb{R}$ where k is any positive integer. Which of the following must be TRUE?

   I. If A is closed, then A is compact.

   II. If for each sequence $\{a_k\}$ with terms in A there is a strictly increasing function $\alpha : \mathbb{Z} \to \mathbb{Z}$ such that $\lim_{k \to \infty} a_{\alpha(k)}$ is in A, then A is compact.

   III. If $B = \bigcup_{k=1}^{\infty} A_k$, then $\overline{B} = \bigcup_{k=1}^{\infty} \overline{A_k}$.

(A) I only

(B) II only

(C) III only

(D) II and III only

(E) I, II, and III

---

59. The probability that a point (x, y) in $\mathbb{R}^2$ is chosen follows a uniform random distribution within the region described by the inequality $0 < |x| + |y| < 1$. What is the probability that $2(x + y) > 1$?

(A) 0   (B) $\dfrac{1}{4}$ (C) $\dfrac{\sqrt{2}}{4}$ (D) $\dfrac{1}{\sqrt{2}}$ (E) $\dfrac{3}{4}$

---

60. Let $\mathbf{F} = \left\langle y, -x, \dfrac{3}{\pi} \right\rangle$ be a vector field in xyz-space. What is the work done by $\mathbf{F}$ on a particle that moves along the path described by $\mathbf{r}(t) = \langle \cos t, \sin t, t^2 \rangle$ where t goes from 0 to $\dfrac{\pi}{2}$?

(A) $-\dfrac{\pi}{2}$ (B) $-\dfrac{\pi}{4}$ (C) 0   (D) $\dfrac{\pi}{4}$ (E) $\dfrac{\pi}{2}$

---

61. There are 25 suitcases, 5 of which are damaged. Three suitcases are selected at random. What is the probability that exactly 2 are damaged?

(A) $\dfrac{2}{69}$

(B) $\dfrac{1}{30}$

(C) $\dfrac{2}{23}$

(D) $\dfrac{12}{125}$

(E) $\dfrac{3}{25}$

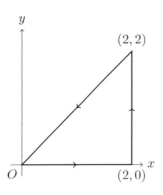

62. Let C be the positively oriented path shown above. Then $\oint_C x\sin(x^2)\,dx + (3e^{y^2} - 2x)\,dy =$

(A) -4 (B) -2 (C) 0 (D) 2 (E) 4

63. The point on the plane $3x - 2y + z = 4$ closest to the origin is

(A) $(1, 2, 5)$

(B) $\left(\dfrac{6}{7}, -\dfrac{2}{7}, \dfrac{6}{7}\right)$

(C) $\left(\dfrac{5}{6}, \dfrac{4}{3}, \dfrac{25}{6}\right)$

(D) $(1, -3, -5)$

(E) $\left(\dfrac{6}{7}, -\dfrac{4}{7}, \dfrac{2}{7}\right)$

64. For each positive integer n, let f_n be the function defined on the interval $[0, 1]$ by $f_n(x) = \dfrac{nx}{1 + nx^2}$. Which of the following statements are TRUE?

   I. The sequence $\{f_n\}$ converges point-wise on $[0, 1]$ to a limit function f .

   II. The sequence $\{f_n\}$ converges uniformly on $[0, 1]$ to a limit function f .

   III. $\left| \displaystyle\int_0^1 f_n(x)\,dx - \int_{\frac{1}{n}}^1 \lim_{k\to\infty} f_k(x)\,dx \right| \to 0$ as $n \to \infty$.

(A) I only

(B) III only

(C) I and II only

(D) I and III only

(E) I, II, and III

GO ON TO THE NEXT PAGE.

---

65. The pattern in the figure above continues infinitely into the page. If the outer most square has sides of length 1, what is the total gray area of the figure?

(A) $1 - \dfrac{\pi}{4}$

(B) $2 - \dfrac{\pi}{3}$

(C) $2 - \dfrac{\pi}{2}$

(D) $\dfrac{1}{2}$

(E) $\dfrac{1 + \pi}{4}$

GO ON TO THE NEXT PAGE.

·	1	i	j	k
1	1	i	j	k
i	i	−1	k	−j
j	j	−k	−1	i
k	k	j	−i	−1

66. Suppose multiplication between 1, **i**, **j**, and **k** are as defined above. Which of the following are rings?

  I. $\{a + b\sqrt[3]{4} : a \text{ and } b \text{ are rational}\}$

 II. The set of functions $f : \mathbb{R} \to \mathbb{R}$ under the standard function addition and multiplication defined by composition

III. $\{a + b\mathbf{i} + c\mathbf{j} + d\mathbf{k} : a, b, c, \text{ and } d \text{ are real}\}$

(A) I only

(B) III only

(C) I and III only

(D) II and III only

(E) I, II, and III

STOP
If you finished before time is called, you may check your work on this test.

Chapter 2

Practice Test 2

The problems begin on the next page. To save paper, less space is provided within this booklet than what is allotted on official GRE mathematics subject tests. You will need your own scratch paper. If you would like to simulate the actual test-taking experience, you will need a scantron. We encourage you to attempt the test while timed because time management skills are critical for success on the GRE. Hang loose!

MATHEMATICS TEST
Time—170 minutes
66 Questions

Directions: Each of the questions or incomplete statements below is followed by five suggested answers or completions. In each case, select the one that is best and then completely fill in the corresponding space on the answer sheet.

Computation and scratch work may be done on a separate sheet of paper.

In this test:

(1) All logarithms with an unspecified base are natural logarithms, that is, with base e.

(2) The symbols $\mathbb{Z}$, $\mathbb{Q}$, $\mathbb{R}$, and $\mathbb{C}$ denote the sets of integers, rational numbers, real numbers, and complex numbers, respectively.

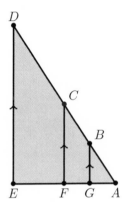

---

1. In the figure above, DE, CF, and BG are parallel, and $EF = 2FG = 2AG$. If the area of trapezoid $CDEF$ is 9, the the area of triangle ADE is

(A) $\dfrac{81}{10}$ (B) $\dfrac{54}{5}$ (C) 12 (D) $\dfrac{81}{5}$ (E) 24

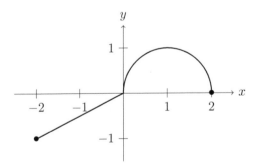

---

2. If the graph above represents f, then $\displaystyle\int_{-2}^{1} f(x)\, dx =$

(A) $\dfrac{\pi - 4}{4}$ (B) $\pi - 1$ (C) $\dfrac{\pi - 2}{2}$ (D) $2\pi - 2$ (E) $2\pi - 1$

GO ON TO THE NEXT PAGE.

3. $\lim\limits_{n \to \infty} e^{-n} \sqrt{e^{n+1} + 1} - e^{-(n+1)} \sqrt{e^n + 1} =$

(A) $-\infty$　　(B) $-e^2$　　(C) $-e$　　(D) 0　　(E) e

4. At how many points in the first quadrant do the graphs of $y = e^x$ and $y = 3 \sin \pi x$ intersect?

(A) Zero　　(B) One　　(C) Two　　(D) Three　　(E) Four

5. Suppose U_1 and U_2 are 5-dimensional subspaces of an 8-dimensional vector space V. The dimension of $U_1 \cap U_2$ CANNOT equal

(A) 1　　(B) 2　　(C) 3　　(D) 4　　(E) 5　　$5+5 - U_1 \cap U_2 \leq 8$

6. An equation of the plane in $\mathbb{R}^3$ which contains the points $(1,0,0)$, $(2,2,0)$, and $(1,0,1)$ is

(A) $-2x + y = 2$　　(B) $2x - y = 2$　　(C) $2x + y = 2$　　(D) $2x - 2y - 2z = 2$　　(E) $2x + 2y - 2z = 2$

7. The tangent line of $f(x) = x^3 - 3x^2 + 5$ at the inflection point of the graph of f makes a triangle with the x- and y-axes. What is the area of the triangle?

(A) 2　　(B) $\dfrac{5}{2}$　　(C) 6　　(D) $\dfrac{7}{2}$　　(E) 10

8. Let $f(x) = x\left(e^{-x} + x\right)$. The 100th derivative $f^{(100)}(x) =$

(A) $xe^{-x} - 100e^{-x}$

(B) $100e^{-x} - xe^{-x}$

(C) xe^{-x}

(D) $xe^{-x} - 101e^{-x}$

(E) $101e^{-x} - xe^{-x}$

$f'(x) = \left(e^{-x} + x\right)\left(-e^{-x}\right) + \left(e^{-x} + x\right) = -2e^{-x}$

9. The geometric object in the complex plane which is described by the relationship

$$|z|^2 = \overline{-iz}$$

is what?

(A) One point　　(B) Two points　　(C) A ray　　(D) A line　　(E) A circle

10. If $f(3) = 5$, $f(10) = 1$, and $\displaystyle\int_3^{10} f(x)\,dx = 20$, then $\displaystyle\int_1^5 f^{-1}(x)\,dx =$

(A) 5　　(B) 12　　(C) 13　　(D) 25　　(E) 31

GO ON TO THE NEXT PAGE.

11. Consider the two series

$$A = \sum_{n=1}^{\infty} a_n \quad \text{and} \quad B = \sum_{n=1}^{\infty} b_n \ .$$

If a_n and b_n are positive for all n, which of the follow are TRUE?

   I. If $\lim_{n \to \infty} \dfrac{a_n}{b_n} = \infty$ and A converges, then B converges.

   II. If $\lim_{n \to \infty} n a_n = 0$, then A converges.

   III. If A converges, then $\displaystyle\sum_{n=1}^{\infty} \dfrac{\sqrt{a_n}}{1 + a_n}$ converges.

(A) I only

(B) II only

(C) III only

(D) I and III only

(E) I, II, and III

12. The graph of the function f contains the point $(1, 1)$. If f satisfies the differential equation

$$\frac{dy}{dx} = x^3 - y,$$

then which of the following is FALSE?

(A) $f(2) = \dfrac{2e + 3}{e}$

(B) $f'(2) = \dfrac{6e - 3}{e}$

(C) The graph of f has a local minimum at $(1, 1)$.

(D) There are no local minima.

(E) The function f is infinitely differentiable.

13. The domain of the real-valued function $f(x) = \log(\tan x)$ is

(A) $\mathbb{R}$

(B) $\displaystyle\bigcup_{n \in \mathbb{Z}} \left(\pi n, \frac{\pi}{2} + \pi n \right)$

(C) $\displaystyle\bigcup_{n \in \mathbb{Z}} \left(\frac{\pi}{2} + \pi n, \pi n + \pi \right)$

(D) $\displaystyle\bigcup_{n \in \mathbb{Z}} \left(\pi n, \pi n + \pi \right)$

(E) $\displaystyle\bigcup_{n \in \mathbb{Z}} \left[\frac{\pi}{2} + \pi n, \pi n + \pi \right)$

GO ON TO THE NEXT PAGE.

14. Let $A = \begin{pmatrix} 2 & -4 \\ -4 & 2 \end{pmatrix}$. The sum of the eigenvalues of A is

(A) 2   (B) 4   (C) 6   (D) 8   (E) 10

$\begin{vmatrix} 2-\lambda & -4 \\ -4 & 2-\lambda \end{vmatrix}$

$(2-\lambda)(2-\lambda) - 16$

$4 - 4\lambda + \lambda^2 - 16$

$\lambda^2 - 4\lambda - 12$

$(\lambda+6)(\lambda-2)$

$\lambda = -6$
$\lambda = 2$

15. Suppose

$$f(x) = \begin{cases} x^2 - 2x + 1, & \text{if } x \le 1 \\ ax + b, & \text{if } x > 1 \end{cases}.$$

If the inverse of f is a function, then a and b could be which of the following?

(A) $a = -2$ and $b = 1$

(B) $a = -1$ and $b = 3$

(C) $a = 0$ and $b = -1$

(D) $a = 1$ and $b = -2$

(E) $a = 2$ and $b = 0$

16. If $x^{100} - 5x^{88} + x - 4$ is divided by $x^2 - 1$, the remainder is

(A) -7 (B) 0   (C) $2 - x$ (D) $x - 8$ (E) $2x - 1$

17. $\displaystyle\sum_{n=0}^{\infty} \left(\frac{1}{2}\right)^{n+3} \frac{1}{n+3} =$

(A) $-\dfrac{5}{8} - \log\dfrac{3}{2}$ (B) $-\dfrac{5}{8} + \log 2$ (C) $-\dfrac{3}{8} + \log\dfrac{3}{2}$ (D) $\dfrac{3}{8} + \log 2$ (E) $\dfrac{5}{8} + \log\dfrac{3}{2}$

18. You want to buy a small box of chocolates for your special someone. There are five types of chocolates to choose from and six chocolates fit in a box. You may put as many of each type of chocolate in the box as will fit and you may choose to omit any type of chocolate. The box must be full. If the order the chocolates are arranged in the box is irrelevant, how many unique boxes of chocolates can you make?

(A) $\binom{10}{4}$

(B) $\binom{10}{5}$

(C) $\binom{11}{4}$

(D) $\binom{11}{6}$

(E) 5^6

GO ON TO THE NEXT PAGE.

19. When the substitution $y = ux$ is applied to the differential equation

$$(x^2 - xy)\frac{dy}{dx} + y^2 = -x^2,$$

the result is equivalent to which of the following within some suitable domain? Do NOT solve the differential equation.

(A) $\dfrac{du}{dx} = \dfrac{u+1}{x(u-1)}$

(B) $\dfrac{du}{dx} = \dfrac{u+1}{x(1-u)}$

(C) $\dfrac{du}{dx} = \dfrac{1}{x}$

(D) $\dfrac{du}{dx} = \dfrac{2u^2 - u + 1}{x(u-1)}$

(E) $\dfrac{du}{dx} = \dfrac{2u^2 - u + 1}{x(1-u)}$

---

20. Suppose $f(x) = ax^2 + bx + c$, where $a > 0$. If the vertex of f has an x-coordinate of 2 and $f(t) < f(-1)$, which of the following are TRUE?

   I. $-1 < t < 5$

   II. $f(t) > f(5)$

   III. $f'(0) = -f'(4)$

(A) I only

(B) II only

(C) III only

(D) I and III only

(E) I, II, and III

---

21. Let $\displaystyle\int_0^1 f(x)\, dx = 3$. Then $\displaystyle\int_1^6 2f\left(\frac{1}{5}(x-1)\right) - 10 \, dx =$

(A) -80 (B) $-\dfrac{244}{5}$ (C) -44 (D) -20 (E) 44

---

22. $\displaystyle\int_0^1 \int_y^1 e^{x^2}\, dx\, dy =$

(A) $\dfrac{1-e}{2}$ (B) $\dfrac{e-1}{2}$ (C) $\dfrac{e}{2}$ (D) $\dfrac{e^2-1}{2}$ (E) $\dfrac{e^2}{2}$

GO ON TO THE NEXT PAGE.

23. The volume of the solid generated by revolving the region bounded above by $y = \sqrt{x}$ and below by $y = \dfrac{4}{\pi} \arctan x$ about the y-axis is

(A) $\dfrac{20 - 6\pi}{5}$ (B) $\dfrac{20\sqrt{2} - 4\pi}{5}$ (C) $\dfrac{20\sqrt{2} - \pi}{5}$ (D) $\dfrac{20\sqrt{2} + \pi}{5}$ (E) $\dfrac{20 + 4\pi}{5}$

24. Which of the following is an equation of a circle tangent to the line with equation $3x + y = 10$?

(A) $x^2 + y^2 = 2$ (B) $x^2 + y^2 = 4$ (C) $x^2 + y^2 = 6$ (D) $x^2 + y^2 = 8$ (E) $x^2 + y^2 = 10$

25. At a particular university, 200 students are registered as math majors. There are

- 100 taking real analysis,
- 50 taking linear algebra,
- 90 taking abstract algebra,
- 40 taking real analysis and linear algebra,
- 75 taking real analysis and abstract algebra,
- 15 taking linear algebra and abstract algebra, and
- 3 taking all three courses.

How many math majors are taking none of the three courses?

(A) 12 (B) 43 (C) 57 (D) 78 (E) 87

26. $\left(\dfrac{\sqrt{3}}{2} - \dfrac{i}{2} \right)^{50} =$

(A) $\dfrac{1}{2} + \dfrac{i\sqrt{3}}{2}$ (B) $\dfrac{1}{2} - \dfrac{i\sqrt{3}}{2}$ (C) $\dfrac{\sqrt{3}}{2} + \dfrac{i}{2}$ (D) $\dfrac{\sqrt{3}}{2} - \dfrac{i}{2}$ (E) $-\dfrac{\sqrt{3}}{2} - \dfrac{i}{2}$

27. If $y = 3x^{x^2}$, then $y' =$

(A) $1 + 2\log x$ (B) $1 - 2\log x$ (C) $3x^{x^2+1}\left(1 + 2\log x\right)$ (D) $3x^{x^2}\left(1 - 2\log x\right)$ (E) $3x^{x^2+1}\left(1 - 2\log x\right)$

28. How many abelian (commutative) groups are there of order 36?

(A) Two (B) Four (C) Six (D) Eight (E) Ten

GO ON TO THE NEXT PAGE.

29. Three distinct integers are chosen randomly from the set $\{1, 2, 3, 4, 5, 6, 7, 8, 9, 10\}$. If $2 \le n \le 9$, the probability that the middle value of the three chosen integers is n must be

(A) $\dfrac{(n-1)(10-n)}{720}$

(B) $\dfrac{(n-1)(10-n)}{120}$

(C) $\dfrac{n(n-1)(10-n)}{720}$

(D) $\dfrac{n(n-1)(10-n)}{120}$

(E) $\dfrac{(n-1)(9-n)(10-n)}{720}$

---

30. Suppose H_1 and H_2 are distinct subgroups of G. If the orders of H_1 and H_2 are both the prime number p, which of the following are true?

I. The prime number p divides the order of G.

II. The subgroups H_1 and H_2 are abelian (commutative).

III. The set $H_1 \cap H_2$ only contains one element.

(A) I only

(B) II only

(C) III only

(D) I and II only

(E) I, II, and III

---

31. If 12 divides $7x + 5y$, then 12 must divide

(A) $11x + y$ (B) $2x + 10y + 1$ (C) $6x + 5y$ (D) $x + y + 10$ (E) $4x + y$

---

32. A point is chosen randomly within the rectangle $\{(x, y) \in \mathbb{R}^2 : -1 < x < 5 \text{ and } -1 < y < 1\}$. What is the probability that the distance between the point $(0, 0)$ and a random point in the rectangle is less than or equal to 2 but greater than 1? Assume each point is equally likely to be selected.

(A) $\dfrac{1 + \sqrt{3} - \pi}{6}$ (B) $\dfrac{6 + 3\sqrt{3} - \pi}{36}$ (C) $\dfrac{6 + 3\sqrt{3} + \pi}{36}$ (D) $\dfrac{2 + \sqrt{3} + \pi}{12}$ (E) $\dfrac{2 + 3\sqrt{3} + 2\pi}{12}$

GO ON TO THE NEXT PAGE.

33. The polynomial $f(x)$ has the smallest degree for which it can have integer coefficients and root (zero) $\sqrt{1-\sqrt{3}}$. If the leading coefficient of $f(x)$ is 1, then $f(x) =$

(A) $x^4 - 2x^2 - 2$ (B) $x^3 - 2x^2 + 3$ (C) $x^4 + 2x^2 - 2$ (D) $x^3 + 2x^2 + 3$ (E) $x^4 + 2x^2 + 2$

34. Let $L(\theta)$ be the arc length from $t = 0$ to $t = \theta$ of the curve in the xy-plane defined by $x = e^{-t}\cos t$ and $y = e^{-t}\sin t$. Then $\lim\limits_{\theta \to \infty} L(\theta) =$

(A) 1   (B) $\dfrac{(e-1)\sqrt{2}}{e}$ (C) $\sqrt{2}$ (D) e (E) $(1+e)\sqrt{2}$

35. A curve in the xy-plane is defined by

$$x = t^2 - 3t$$
$$y = 3t - t^3$$

for all t in $\mathbb{R}$. The value of $\dfrac{d^2y}{dx^2}$ at the point $(-2, 2)$ is

(A) -8 (B) -6 (C) -4 (D) -2 (E) 0

36. If x is in $\mathbb{Z}_{11}$ and

$$2x \equiv \frac{3x + 7}{x^{10} + 1} \pmod{11},$$

then $x =$

(A) 1   (B) 4   (C) 7   (D) 10   (E) 13

37. Consider the ring of integers $\mathbb{Z}$ under the standard definitions of addition and multiplication. An ideal is a subring I of $\mathbb{Z}$ such that for each m in $\mathbb{Z}$, we have $mI \subseteq I$. Denote the smallest ideal which contains m by (m) . Which of the following are TRUE?

   I. The set $(m) + (n) = \{k + \ell : k \in (m) \text{ and } \ell \in (n)\}$ is an ideal and is equal to (d), where d is the greatest common factor of m and n .

   II. The set $(m) \cdot (n) = \{k \cdot \ell : k \in (m) \text{ and } \ell \in (n)\}$ is an ideal and is equal to (mn) .

   III. The only ideals of $\mathbb{Z}$ are of the form $m\mathbb{Z} = \{mk : k \in \mathbb{Z}\}$, where m is an integer.

(A) I only

(B) II only

(C) I and II only

(D) II and III only

(E) I, II, and III

38. The slope field of

$$\frac{dy}{dx} = -\frac{x}{y}$$

is

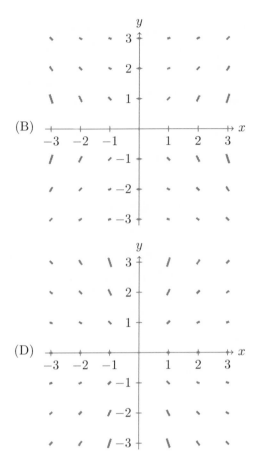

39. The point on the surface of the unit-ball which is closest to the plane $3x - 12y + 4z = 9$ has coordinates

(A) $\left(\dfrac{1}{3}, -\dfrac{2}{3}, \dfrac{2}{3}\right)$

(B) $\left(-\dfrac{1}{3}, \dfrac{2}{3}, -\dfrac{2}{3}\right)$

(C) $\left(-\dfrac{3}{13}, \dfrac{12}{13}, -\dfrac{4}{13}\right)$

(D) $\left(\dfrac{3}{13}, -\dfrac{12}{13}, \dfrac{4}{13}\right)$

(E) $\left(-\dfrac{2}{7}, \dfrac{3}{7}, -\dfrac{6}{7}\right)$

40. If A and B are $n \times n$ matrices with entries in $\mathbb{R}$, then which of the following are TRUE?

I. If $A = A^T$ and $\mathrm{tr}(A^2) = 0$, then $A = 0$.

II. If $AB = -BA$ and both A and B are invertible, then n is even.

III. If there are integers n and m such that $A^n = 0$ and $B^m = 0$, then $A + B$ is not invertible.

(A) I only

(B) II only

(C) I and II only

(D) III only

(E) I, II, and III

41. Suppose $f(x) = 8 \log x$. Which of the following is closest to $f(1.5)$?

(A) 2.5   (B) 3   (C) 3.5   (D) 4   (E) 4.5

GO ON TO THE NEXT PAGE.

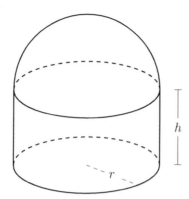

42. You would like to build a silo to store precisely 48π m^3 of ramen noodles for graduate school. The silo is comprised of a cylinder of radius r and height h which has a closed circular base and a roof in the form of an upper hemisphere (i.e. the top half of a sphere). If the floor costs $6/\pi$ per m^2, the sides cost $3/\pi$ per m^2, and the roof costs $8/\pi$ per m^2, what is the radius that minimizes cost?

(A) $r = 1$ m   (B) $r = 2$ m   (C) $r = 3$ m   (D) $r = 4$ m   (E) $r = 5$ m

43. The vector valued function $\mathbf{r} : \mathbb{R} \to \mathbb{R}^2$ describes a curve on the xy-plane such that $\mathbf{r}(0) = \langle -1, 0 \rangle$ and $\mathbf{r}'(0) = \langle 1, 2 \rangle$. If $f(x, y) = x \sin y$, then

$$\frac{d}{dt}\Big(f\left(\mathbf{r}(t)\right) \Big)\bigg|_{t=0} =$$

(A) -2 (B) -1   (C) 0   (D) 1   (E) 2

44. Consider the following algorithm, which takes an input integer **n** > 0, and prints a real number.

```
input(n)
  begin
      set h = 1/n
      set x = 0
      set S = 0
    while x < 1
      begin
         replace x = x + h
         replace S = S + x*x*h
      end
    print S
  end
```

If the input is **n** = 100000, which number would be closest to the value printed?

(A) 0   (B) $\dfrac{1}{4}$ (C) $\dfrac{1}{3}$ (D) $\dfrac{1}{2}$ (E) $\dfrac{3}{4}$

45. Let $A = \begin{pmatrix} 0 & 0 & 1 \\ 1 & 0 & 0 \\ 0 & 1 & 0 \end{pmatrix}$. Then A^{500} is

(A) $\begin{pmatrix} 0 & 1 & 0 \\ 1 & 0 & 1 \\ 0 & 0 & 1 \end{pmatrix}$

(B) $\begin{pmatrix} 0 & 1 & 0 \\ 0 & 0 & 1 \\ 1 & 0 & 0 \end{pmatrix}$

(C) $\begin{pmatrix} 1 & 0 & 0 \\ 0 & 1 & 0 \\ 0 & 0 & 1 \end{pmatrix}$

(D) $\begin{pmatrix} 0 & 0 & 1 \\ 1 & 0 & 0 \\ 0 & 1 & 0 \end{pmatrix}$

(E) $\begin{pmatrix} 1 & 0 & 0 \\ 1 & 0 & 0 \\ 0 & 1 & 0 \end{pmatrix}$

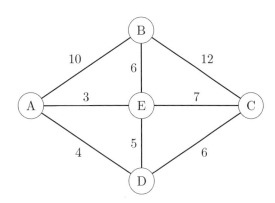

46. The figure above shows an undirected graph with five vertices, and the weights of each of the edges. A spanning tree is a connected subgraph having the same number of vertices and no cycles. The minimum sum of the weights of a spanning tree is

(A) 17   (B) 19   (C) 25   (D) 31   (E) 35

47. Let C be the circle $x^2 + y^2 = 4$ oriented counterclockwise in the xy-plane. If $\mathbf{F} = \langle \sin x^2 + y, 2x \rangle$, what is the value of the line integral $\oint_C \mathbf{F} \cdot d\mathbf{s}$?

(A) 0   (B) 1   (C) 2π (D) 4π (E) 8π

GO ON TO THE NEXT PAGE.

48. What is the dimension of the subspace of $\mathbb{R}^4$ spanned by the vectors in the set

$$\left\{ \begin{pmatrix} 1 \\ 1 \\ 1 \\ 0 \end{pmatrix}, \begin{pmatrix} 0 \\ -2 \\ 0 \\ 0 \end{pmatrix}, \begin{pmatrix} 1 \\ 0 \\ 1 \\ 0 \end{pmatrix}, \begin{pmatrix} \pi \\ \pi \\ \pi \\ \pi \end{pmatrix}, \begin{pmatrix} 0 \\ 0 \\ 5 \\ 5 \end{pmatrix} \right\} ?$$

(A) 1   (B) 2   (C) 3   (D) 4   (E) 5

49. Forces $\mathbf{F}_1$ and $\mathbf{F}_2$ are applied to an object, and have magnitudes 5 and 10 pounds, respectively. The resultant force has a magnitude of 12 pounds. If the angle between $\mathbf{F}_1$ and $\mathbf{F}_2$ is θ, then $\cos\theta =$

(A) $\dfrac{7}{100}$ (B) $\dfrac{19}{100}$ (C) $\dfrac{21}{100}$ (E) $\dfrac{33}{100}$

50. The function f is twice-differentiable and real-valued on $\mathbb{R}$. An application of the trapezoidal rule to approximate $\displaystyle\int_0^1 f(x)\,dx$ results in an underestimate and an approximation of $\displaystyle\int_0^1 f(x)\,dx$ using a left Riemann sum results in an overestimate. Which of the following could be the graph of $y = f(x)$?

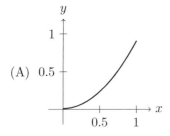

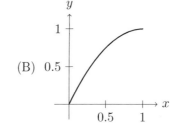

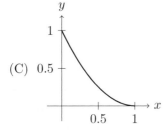

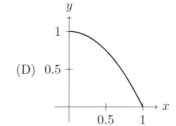

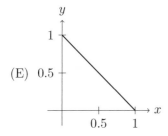

GO ON TO THE NEXT PAGE.

51. A tank initially contains 200 liters of fresh water. A salt solution of concentration 10 grams of salt per liter of water is pumped into the tank at a rate of 10 liters per minute. The solution is perfectly mixed into the tank's water. The solution is then pumped out at a rate of 10 liters per minute. How many grams of salt are in the tank after 60 minutes?

(A) 2000

(B) $2000 - 2000e^{-3}$

(C) $2000 + 2000e^{-3}$

(D) $2000 - 2000e^{-6}$

(E) $2000 + 2000e^{-6}$

---

52. The permutation $\sigma = (1,2,3)(4,5)$ is an element of S_6, where S_6 is the group of symmetries of the set $\{1,2,3,4,5,6\}$. For example, $\sigma(1) = 2$, $\sigma(3) = 1$, $\sigma(5) = 4$, and $\sigma(6) = 6$. The element σ^{75} is equal to which of the following?

(A) The identity   (B) $(4,5)$ (C) $(1,2,3)$ (D) $(1,3,2)$ (E) $(1,3,2)(4,5)$

---

53. Suppose that A, B, C, and D are statements. The statement D is true if

- either A or B is true but not both, or
- statement C is false and both A and B are true.

If D is false, then which of the following is the strongest claim?

(A) A and B are both false

(B) C is true or A and B are both false

(C) C is true and A and B have the same truth value

(D) C is true or A and B have the same truth value

(E) C is true and A and B are both true

---

54. Suppose the probability that a nonnegative integer n occurs is $p(n)$ and $p(n+1) = \dfrac{2}{3}p(n)$. The probability that $n < 0$ or n is not an integer is zero. What is the probability that n is greater than two?

(A) $\dfrac{27}{64}$ (B) $\dfrac{8}{27}$ (C) $\dfrac{9}{16}$ (D) $\dfrac{4}{9}$ (E) $\dfrac{3}{4}$

55. A function $f : \mathbb{R} \to \mathbb{R}$ is convex if for each t in the closed interval $[0, 1]$ and x and y in $\mathbb{R}$, we have

$$f\left(tx + (1 - t)y\right) \leq tf(x) + (1 - t)f(y) \ .$$

Which of the following are TRUE?

   I. The function $g(x) = x^2$ is convex.

  II. Suppose x is in $\mathbb{R}$ and $0 \leq t \leq 1$. If f is a convex function and $f(0) \leq 0$, then $f(tx) \leq tf(x)$.

 III. The second derivative of a convex function exists and is nonnegative.

(A) I only

(B) II only

(C) I and II only

(D) III

(E) I, II, and III only

---

56. If $f(x, y) = x^4y^2 + 4xy^2 - 12y + 5$ for all real numbers x and y, then

(A) f has a relative maximum at $(1, 2)$.

(B) f has a relative minimum at $(1, -2)$.

(C) f has a saddle point at $(-1, -2)$.

(D) f has an absolute maximum at $(-1, -2)$.

(E) f has a critical point on the line $y = 0$.

GO ON TO THE NEXT PAGE.

57. The dyadic rationals are defined to be the set

$$D = \left\{ \frac{m}{2^n} : \; m \text{ and } n \text{ are integers} \right\} \; .$$

Which of the following are TRUE?

I. There is a one-to-one function f which maps D <u>onto</u> $\mathbb{R}$.

II. The closure of the dyadic rationals $\overline{D}$ is equal to $\mathbb{R}$.

III. The sequence $\{f_n\}$ defined by

$$f_n(x) = \begin{cases} 1, & \text{if } x = \dfrac{m}{2^n} \text{ and } m \in \mathbb{N} \\ \dfrac{1}{2^n}, & \text{otherwise} \end{cases}$$

converges uniformly to

$$f(x) = \begin{cases} 1, & \text{if } x \in D \\ 0, & \text{otherwise} \end{cases}$$

on the closed interval $[0, 1]$.

(A) I only

(B) II only

(C) I and II only

(D) III only

(E) II and III only

---

58. A fair coin is flipped 400 times. What is the probability that the number of heads is no more than 185?

(A) Less than 2.4%

(B) Between 2.4% and 15.9%

(C) Between 15.9% and 50%

(D) Between 50% and 84%

(E) More than 84%

GO ON TO THE NEXT PAGE.

59. Suppose the set X contains an infinite number of points and the collection of open subsets of X is

$$\mathcal{T} = \{U \subseteq X : U = \varnothing \text{ or } U^c \text{ is finite}\},$$

where U^c denotes the complement of U . Which of the following are TRUE?

   I. If U is an infinite subset of X, then the closure $\overline{U} = X$.

  II. If f is a continuous real-valued function on X, then f is constant.

 III. For each x_1 and x_2 in X there exist U_1 and U_2 in $\mathcal{T}$ such that $x_1 \in U_1$, $x_2 \in U_2$, and $U_1 \cap U_2 = \varnothing$.

(A) I only

(B) II only

(C) I and II only

(D) III

(E) I, II, and III

60. If $\begin{vmatrix} a & b & c \\ d & e & f \\ g & h & i \end{vmatrix} = 1$, then $\begin{vmatrix} 2a - 3d & -d & g - 6a + 9d \\ 2b - 3e & -e & h - 6b + 9e \\ 2c - 3f & -f & i - 6c + 9f \end{vmatrix} =$

(A) -4 (B) -3 (C) -2 (D) -1 (E) 0

61. Which of the following are vector spaces over the field $\mathbb{R}$?

   I. The vectors $\mathbf{v}$ whose tails are on the origin and whose tips are on the plane

$$3x - 2y + 10z = 0$$

  II. The set of $\mathbf{x}$ in $\mathbb{R}^n$ such that $\mathbf{x}$ is a solution of $A\mathbf{x} = \mathbf{0}$, where A is an $m \times n$ matrix with real coefficients

 III. The set of real-valued and twice differentiable functions f such that $y = f(x)$ is a solution of

$$y'' = x(y' + y + 1)$$

(A) I only

(B) II only

(C) I and II only

(D) III only

(E) I, II, and III

GO ON TO THE NEXT PAGE.

62. Let f be an analytic function of the complex variable $z = x + iy$, where x and y are real variables, such that
$$f(z) = g(x, y) + 6ixy,$$
and $g(0,0) = 0$, then $g(1, -1) =$

(A) -6 (B) -3 (C) 0 (D) 3 (E) 6

---

63. Define
$$f(x) = \int_0^x \sin t^2 \, dt \ .$$

Which of the following are TRUE?

I. $f'\left(\dfrac{\sqrt{\pi}}{2}\right) = \dfrac{\sqrt{2}}{2}$

II. $\lim\limits_{x \to 0} \dfrac{f(x)}{x^3} = \dfrac{1}{3}$

III. $\displaystyle\int_{\sqrt{\pi}/2}^{\sqrt{2\pi}/2} f(x) \, dx = \dfrac{\sqrt{2\pi}}{2} f\left(\dfrac{\sqrt{2\pi}}{2}\right) - \dfrac{\sqrt{\pi}}{2} f\left(\dfrac{\sqrt{\pi}}{2}\right) - \dfrac{\sqrt{2}}{4}$

(A) I only

(B) II only

(C) III only

(D) I and III only

(E) I, II, and III

GO ON TO THE NEXT PAGE.

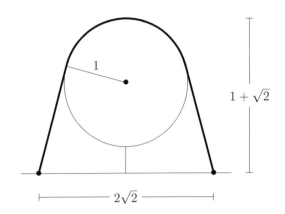

---

64. The thick band in the figure above has length

(A) $\dfrac{5\pi}{6} - \sqrt{3}$ (B) $2\sqrt{3} - \dfrac{2\pi}{3}$ (C) $\dfrac{5\pi}{6} + \sqrt{3}$ (D) $\dfrac{2\pi}{3} + 2\sqrt{3}$ (E) $\dfrac{5\pi}{6} + 2\sqrt{3}$

---

65. If S is the surface of the cube whose main diagonal has endpoints $(0,0,0)$ and $(1,1,1)$, and the vector field $\mathbf{F}(x,y,z) = \langle z,y,z \rangle$ for all (x,y,z) in $\mathbb{R}^3$, then what is the value of the flux of the vector field $\mathbf{F}(x,y,x)$ through S given that S has outward orientation?

(A) -1   (B) 0   (C) 1   (D) 2   (E) 3

---

66. For all x and y in $\mathbb{R}$ the real-valued function f satisfies

$$|f(x) - f(y)| \le |x - y|^2 \ .$$

Which of the following are TRUE?

   I. The function f is continuous on its entire domain.

   II. There is a constant C such that $|f(x) - f(y)| \le C\,|x - y|$.

   III. The function f is differentiable.

(A) I only

(B) II only

(C) II only

(D) I and III only

(E) I, II, and III

STOP
If you finished before time is called, you may check your work on this test.

Chapter 3

Answers

Practice Test 1

1. B		34. A	
2. A		35. A	
3. A		36. C	
4. E		37. E	
5. D		38. A	
6. C		39. E	
7. C		40. C	
8. B		41. B	
9. D		42. D	
10. D		43. A	
11. A		44. D	
12. B		45. A	
13. B		46. E	
14. B		47. E	
15. A		48. A	
16. B		49. D	
17. E		50. A	
18. D		51. E	
19. B		52. D	
20. C		53. E	
21. C		54. C	
22. A		55. A	
23. A		56. C	
24. D		57. C	
25. D		58. B	
26. C		59. B	
27. C		60. D	
28. E		61. C	
29. C		62. A	
30. D		63. E	
31. D		64. A	
32. D		65. C	
33. E		66. B	

Practice Test 2

1.	C	34.	C
2.	A	35.	B
3.	D	36.	C
4.	C	37.	E
5.	A	38.	C
6.	B	39.	D
7.	C	40.	C
8.	A	41.	B
9.	B	42.	B
10.	D	43.	A
11.	A	44.	C
12.	D	45.	B
13.	B	46.	B
14.	B	47.	D
15.	A	48.	D
16.	D	49.	B
17.	B	50.	D
18.	A	51.	B
19.	A	52.	B
20.	D	53.	B
21.	D	54.	B
22.	B	55.	C
23.	A	56.	C
24.	E	57.	B
25.	E	58.	B
26.	B	59.	C
27.	C	60.	C
28.	B	61.	C
29.	B	62.	C
30.	E	63.	E
31.	A	64.	E
32.	B	65.	D
33.	A	66.	E

Chapter 4

Practice Test 1 Solutions

Solution 1.

Two well know *limits* from Calculus are

$$\lim_{x \to 0} \frac{\sin x}{x} = 1 \quad \text{and} \quad \lim_{x \to 0} \frac{1 - \cos x}{x} = 0.$$

Our task is to deconstruct the limit into factors where we can use the above:

$$\lim_{n \to \infty} n \left(1 - \cos \frac{1}{\sqrt{n}} \right) \sin \frac{1}{\sqrt{n}} = \lim_{n \to \infty} \frac{1 - \cos \dfrac{1}{\sqrt{n}}}{\dfrac{1}{\sqrt{n}}} \lim_{n \to \infty} \frac{\sin \dfrac{1}{\sqrt{n}}}{\dfrac{1}{\sqrt{n}}}.$$

If we let $x = 1/\sqrt{n}$, we see that

$$\lim_{n \to \infty} n \left(1 - \cos \frac{1}{\sqrt{n}} \right) \sin \frac{1}{\sqrt{n}} = \lim_{x \to 0^+} \frac{1 - \cos x}{x} \lim_{x \to 0^+} \frac{\sin x}{x} = 0 \cdot 1 = 0.$$

Therefore, the solution is (B). ∎

Solution 2.

We will use *derivative rules* from Calculus to compute g', particularly the product and quotient rules. We have

$$g'(x) = \frac{(x^2 + 1)\Big(f(x^2) + 2x^2 f'(x^2)\Big) - 2x^2 f(x^2)}{(x^2 + 1)^2}.$$

It follows that

$$g'(2) = \frac{5\Big(f(4) + 8f'(4)\Big) - 8f(4)}{25} = \frac{5\Big(3 + 8(-2)\Big) - 8(3)}{25} = -\frac{89}{25}.$$

Alternatively, we could have computed g' for a particular f which satisfies the given criteria, e.g.

$$f(x) = -2x + 11.$$

Regardless of our approach, the solution is (A). ∎

Solution 3.

Let us compute our derivatives:

$$f'(x) = 3x^2 - 6x + 4 \quad \text{and} \quad f''(x) = 6x - 6.$$

It follows that an *inflection point* occurs at $x = 1$ because the second derivative changes signs there.

To find a linear equation, we need a point and a slope. We obtain those respective values through evaluation of $f(1)$ and $f'(1)$:

$$f(1) = 1 - 3 + 4 - 3 = -1 \quad \text{and} \quad f'(1) = 3 - 6 + 4 = 1.$$

Hence, an equation of a line which is tangent to f at the inflection point $(1, -1)$ is $y = x - 2$. Choose (A) and move on! ∎

Solution 4. ──

Using *integration by parts* with $u = \log x$ and $dv = dx$, we see

$$
\int_e^{e^2} \log x \, dx = x \log x \Big|_e^{e^2} - \int_e^{e^2} x \cdot \frac{1}{x} \, dx
$$

$$
= x \log x \Big|_e^{e^2} - \int_e^{e^2} dx
$$

$$
= x \log x - x \Big|_e^{e^2}
$$

$$
= e^2 \log e^2 - e^2 - e \log e + e
$$

$$
= 2e^2 - e^2 - e + e
$$

$$
= e^2.
$$

Thus, the answer is (E). If you are unfamiliar with the *logarithm properties* we used above, see the glossary for details. ∎

Solution 5. ──

Notice that our limit is in the $0/0$ indeterminate form, which means we can use *L'Hôspital's rule*:

$$
\lim_{x \to 1} \frac{f(x) - 2}{(x-1)^2} \overset{LH}{=} \lim_{x \to 1} \frac{f'(x)}{2(x-1)}.
$$

Because

$$
f'(1) = \frac{dy}{dx}\bigg|_{(1,2)} = 1 - \frac{2}{2} = 0,
$$

we are in another $0/0$ indeterminate form. As a result, we will use L'Hôspital's rule a second time:

$$
\lim_{x \to 1} \frac{f'(x)}{2(x-1)} \overset{LH}{=} \lim_{x \to 1} \frac{f''(x)}{2}.
$$

All that is left is to find $f''(x)$. We know

$$
f''(x) = \frac{d}{dx}\left(\frac{dy}{dx}\right) = \frac{d}{dx}\left(x - \frac{y}{2}\right) = 1 - \frac{1}{2}\frac{dy}{dx}.
$$

It follows that

$$
f''(1) = 1 - \frac{1}{2}\frac{dy}{dx}\bigg|_{(1,2)} = 1 - \frac{1}{2}(0) = 1.
$$

Hence,

$$
\lim_{x \to 1} \frac{f(x) - 2}{(x-1)^2} = \lim_{x \to 1} \frac{f''(x)}{2} = \frac{f''(1)}{2} = \frac{1}{2}.
$$

We conclude that (D) is correct. ∎

Solution 6. ──

There is a theorem from linear algebra which says the *volume of a parallelepiped* determined by the vectors **u**, **v**, and **w** is

$$\pm\det\begin{pmatrix}\mathbf{u}\\\mathbf{v}\\\mathbf{w}\end{pmatrix}$$

where the vectors are row vectors and the $\pm$ makes the determinate positive.

We have

$$\det\begin{pmatrix}0 & 2 & 0\\1 & -1 & 0\\-2 & 2 & 1\end{pmatrix}=0\begin{vmatrix}-1 & 0\\2 & 1\end{vmatrix}-2\begin{vmatrix}1 & 0\\-2 & 1\end{vmatrix}+0\begin{vmatrix}1 & -1\\-2 & 2\end{vmatrix}=-2.$$

So, the volume must be 2. Select (C)! ■

Solution 7. ──

Consider the graph of $y=a(x-b)^2+c$. If $a>0$ the parabola opens upward, and if $a<0$ the parabola opens downward. Furthermore, the vertex is (b,c).

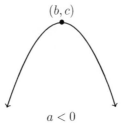
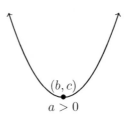

With this in mind, we know that the graph of $y=a(x-b)^2+c$ intersects $y=2$ if

$$a>0 \text{ and } c<2, \quad a<0 \text{ and } c>2, \quad \text{or} \quad a=0 \text{ and } c=2.$$

The only option which satisfies this criteria is (C). ■

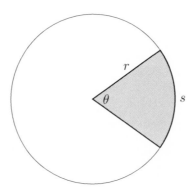

Solution 8. ──

We need two formulas. Suppose θ is the radian measure of the central angle of a circle of radius r. If s is the length of the arc subtended by θ, then $s=r\theta$. If the area of the sector inclosed by s and two radii is A, then $A=r^2\theta/2$.

Imagine that we slice the lateral surface area of our cone along a slant height. The result looks like the following.

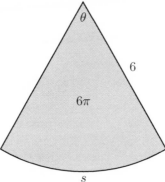

This is a sector whose interior angle θ can be found via the equation

$$\frac{6^2 \theta}{2} = 6\pi \quad \text{implies} \quad \theta = \frac{\pi}{3}.$$

We can find the circumference of the base by computing the arc length

$$s = 6\left(\frac{\pi}{3}\right) = 2\pi.$$

If r is the radius of the base, then

$$2\pi r = 2\pi \quad \text{implies} \quad r = 1.$$

We conclude that the answer is 1, and we pick (B). ∎

Solution 9. ───

Recall that

$$\mathbf{u} \cdot \mathbf{v} = |\mathbf{u}|\,|\mathbf{v}| \cos \theta,$$

where θ is the angle between $\mathbf{u}$ and $\mathbf{v}$.

Let us compute the pieces:

$$\mathbf{u} \cdot \mathbf{v} = 6\sqrt{2} + 0 + 6\sqrt{2} = 12\sqrt{2}, \quad |\mathbf{u}| = \sqrt{2^2 + 2^2} = 2\sqrt{2},$$

and

$$|\mathbf{v}| = \sqrt{\left(3\sqrt{2}\right)^2 + \left(-6\sqrt{3}\right)^2 + \left(3\sqrt{2}\right)^2} = \sqrt{144} = 12.$$

It follows that

$$12\sqrt{2} = (2\sqrt{2})(12)\cos\theta \quad \text{implies} \quad \cos\theta = \frac{1}{2}.$$

The angle measure $\theta = 60°$ satisfies our equation, so we conclude that (D) is correct. ∎

Solution 10.

We know that

$$\dim(U) + \dim(V) - \dim(U \cap V) \le \dim(\mathbb{R}^5) \quad \text{implies} \quad 3 + 3 - \dim(U \cap V) \le 5 \quad \text{implies} \quad \dim(U \cap V) \ge 1.$$

It is not too tough to produce examples where the dimension of $U \cap V$ is 1, 2, or 3. Hence, (D) is the correct answer. ∎

Solution 11.

Since

$$|x + 1| = \begin{cases} x + 1, & \text{if } x \ge -1 \\ -x - 1, & \text{if } x < -1, \end{cases}$$

we see that

$$f(x) = \begin{cases} \dfrac{x^2 - 6x}{1 + x + 1}, & \text{if } x \ge -1 \\ \dfrac{x^2 - 6x}{1 - x - 1}, & \text{if } x < -1. \end{cases} = \begin{cases} \dfrac{x^2 - 6x}{x + 2}, & \text{if } x \ge -1 \\ \text{if } -x + 6, & \text{if } x < -1. \end{cases}$$

It follows that

$$f'(x) = \begin{cases} \dfrac{(x + 2)(2x - 6) - (x^2 - 6x)(1)}{(x + 2)^2}, & \text{if } x > -1 \\ -1, & \text{if } x < -1 \end{cases} = \begin{cases} \dfrac{(x + 6)(x - 2)}{(x + 2)^2}, & \text{if } x > -1 \\ -1, & \text{if } x < -1. \end{cases}$$

Because

$$\lim_{x \to -1^+} f'(x) = -15 \quad \text{and} \quad \lim_{x \to -1^-} f'(x) = -1,$$

the derivative f' is undefined at $x = -1$, due to the fact that *derivatives have no "simple discontinuities"*. Therefore, our critical numbers are $x = -1$ and $x = 2$.

Using f', we can deduce that f has an absolute minimum. In particular,

$$f'(x) < 0 \quad \text{for} \quad x < -1$$

tells us that f is always decreasing when $x < -1$. Since

$$f'(x) > 0 \quad \text{for} \quad x > 2,$$

we know f is always increasing when $x > 2$.

Let us test our critical points because those are our only candidates for the absolute minimum:

$$f(-1) = \frac{(-1)^2 - 6(-1)}{1 + |-1 + 1|} = 7 \quad \text{and} \quad f(2) = \frac{2^2 - 6(2)}{1 + |2 + 1|} = -2.$$

We conclude that the absolute minimum is -2. Select (A) and continue. ∎

Solution 12. ───

Once we find constants a and b such that

$$a \begin{pmatrix} 1 \\ -3 \end{pmatrix} + b \begin{pmatrix} 1 \\ 1 \end{pmatrix} = \begin{pmatrix} 0 \\ 2 \end{pmatrix},$$

we will be almost done because

$$T \begin{pmatrix} 0 \\ 2 \end{pmatrix} = T \left(a \begin{pmatrix} 1 \\ -3 \end{pmatrix} + b \begin{pmatrix} 1 \\ 1 \end{pmatrix} \right) = aT \begin{pmatrix} 1 \\ -3 \end{pmatrix} + bT \begin{pmatrix} 1 \\ 1 \end{pmatrix} = 5a - 2b.$$

Let us find our a and b:

$$a \begin{pmatrix} 1 \\ -3 \end{pmatrix} + b \begin{pmatrix} 1 \\ 1 \end{pmatrix} = \begin{pmatrix} 0 \\ 2 \end{pmatrix}$$

implies the system

$$\begin{cases} a + b = 0 \\ -3a + b = 2 \end{cases}$$

is true. Solving it gives $a = -1/2$ and $b = 1/2$. Thus,

$$T \begin{pmatrix} 0 \\ 2 \end{pmatrix} = 5 \left(-\frac{1}{2} \right) - 2 \left(\frac{1}{2} \right) = -\frac{7}{2}.$$

The answer must be (B)! ∎

Solution 13. ───

We have

$$f'(x) = -17(1 - x)^{16} e^{2x} + 2(1 - x)^{17} e^{2x}.$$

Similarly

$$f''(x) = 17(16)(1 - x)^{15} e^{2x} - 2(17)(1 - x)^{16} e^{2x} - 2(17)(1 - x)^{16} e^{2x} + 2^2 (1 - x)^{17} e^{2x}$$
$$= 17(16)(1 - x)^{15} e^{2x} - 4(17)(1 - x)^{16} e^{2x} + 2^2 (1 - x)^{17} e^{2x}.$$

From here, we see

$$f^{(k)}(x) = (-1)^k \frac{17!}{(17 - k)!} (1 - x)^{17-k} e^{2x} + \text{other terms}.$$

Since all the "other terms" have factors of $1 - x$ raised to powers greater than $17 - k$,

$$f^{(17)}(1) = (-1)^{17} \frac{17!}{0!} e^2 + 0 = -(17! e^2).$$

Fill in the bubble for (B) and continue. ∎

Solution 14. ───

Consider the worst case scenario:

A student dislikes three classmates and three different classmates dislike this student.

Since this student cannot be teammates with any of the six, there would need to be seven teams to choose from. Therefore, if there are seven teams, we can order the students and place them into teams one-by-one by placing each student into one of the one or more teams in which all the members like each other. Choice (B) must be correct. ∎

Solution 15.

Notice
$$\frac{dy}{dx} < 0 \text{ for } x < 0, \quad \frac{dy}{dx} > 0 \text{ for } x > 0, \quad \text{and} \quad \frac{dy}{dx} = 0 \text{ for } x = 0$$

as long as $y \neq 0$. That leaves (A) and (C).

We can see that
$$\frac{dy}{dx} \to \infty \quad \text{as} \quad x \to \infty,$$

when $y \neq 0$. This eliminates (C). We shade in (A). ∎

Solution 16.

We will use the *inclusion-exclusion principle*. It says the number of elements in the set $A \cup B \cup C$ is

$$|A \cup B \cup C| = |A| + |B| + |C| - |A \cap B| - |A \cap C| - |B \cap C| + |A \cap B \cap C|.$$

Let us find the number of elements in each set. The set I_n is the number of integers divisible by n between 1 and 1000, inclusive. So,

$$|I_6| = \left\lfloor \frac{1000}{6} \right\rfloor = 166, \quad |I_{15}| = \left\lfloor \frac{1000}{15} \right\rfloor = 66, \quad \text{and} \quad |I_{25}| = \left\lfloor \frac{1000}{25} \right\rfloor = 40,$$

where $\lfloor \cdot \rfloor$ denotes the floor function.

The elements of the intersection $I_m \cap I_n$ are those which are divisible by both m and n. A number is divisible by m and n if and only if it is divisible by $\text{lcm}\{m, n\}$ (the least common multiple of m and n), so $I_m \cap I_n$ is the set of multiples of $\text{lcm}\{m, n\}$ which are between 1 and 1000, inclusive. Similarly, the set $I_\ell \cap I_m \cap I_n$ is the set of multiples of $\text{lcm}\{\ell, m, n\}$ between 1 and 1000, inclusive. With this in mind, we have

$$|I_6 \cap I_{15}| = \left\lfloor \frac{1000}{30} \right\rfloor = 33, \quad |I_6 \cap I_{25}| = \left\lfloor \frac{1000}{150} \right\rfloor = 6, \quad |I_{15} \cap I_{25}| = \left\lfloor \frac{1000}{75} \right\rfloor = 13,$$

and $|I_6 \cap I_{15} \cap I_{25}| = \lfloor 1000/150 \rfloor = 6$.

It follows that

$$|I_6 \cup I_{15} \cup I_{25}| = |I_6| + |I_{15}| + |I_{25}| - |I_6 \cap I_{15}| - |I_6 \cap I_{25}| - |I_{15} \cap I_{25}| + |I_6 \cap I_{15} \cap I_{25}|$$
$$= 166 + 66 + 40 - 33 - 6 - 13 + 6$$
$$= 226.$$

This corresponds to (B), so we select it. ∎

Solution 17. ───

Let us compute our integral:

$$\iint_S xy \, dA = \int_{y=1}^{3} \int_{x=0}^{1} xy^2 \, dxdy$$

$$= \int_{1}^{3} y^2 \, dy \int_{0}^{1} x \, dx$$

$$= \left[\frac{y^3}{3}\right]_1^3 \left[\frac{x^2}{2}\right]_0^1$$

$$= \left(\frac{26}{3}\right)\left(\frac{1}{2}\right)$$

$$= \frac{13}{3}.$$

We conclude that (E) is correct. ∎

Solution 18. ───

Option I is false. Consider

$$f(x) := x + 1 \quad \text{and} \quad g(x) := -\frac{1}{x}.$$

Note that, for f,

$$a = 1, \quad b = 1, \quad c = 0, \quad \text{and} \quad d = 1,$$

and, for g,

$$a = 0, \quad b = -1, \quad c = 1, \quad \text{and} \quad d = 0,$$

so both functions satisfy $ad - bc = 1$. Therefore, f and g are in $\mathcal{F}$, but

$$(f \circ g)(x) = -\frac{1}{x} + 1 \quad \text{and} \quad (g \circ f)(x) = -\frac{1}{x+1}.$$

That is, $f \circ g \neq g \circ f$ even though both functions are in $\mathcal{F}$.

Option II is true. The function $i(x) := x$ is in $\mathcal{F}$, because

$$a = 1, \quad b = 0, \quad c = 0, \quad \text{and} \quad d = 1,$$

which satisfies $ad - bc = 1$. Hence, we have a function i in $\mathcal{F}$ such that $f \circ i = i \circ f$ for all f.

Option III is valid. Function composition is associative generally. Therefore, it must be associative in $\mathcal{F}$.

We are ready to make our conclusions. The correct answer must be (D) because II and III are true. Select it and continue! ∎

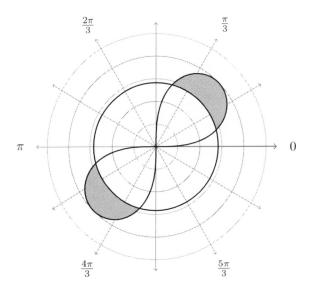

Solution 19.

The area contained within the curve defined by the polar equation $r = f(\theta)$ from $\theta = \alpha$ to $\theta = \beta$ is

$$\frac{1}{2} \int_\alpha^\beta r^2 \, d\theta,$$

when there is no overlapping area.

We need to find where the curves intersect. To do this, we set the curves equal to each other and solve:

$$\left(\sqrt{2}\right)^2 = 4\sin 2\theta \quad \text{implies} \quad \sin 2\theta = \frac{1}{2} \quad \text{implies} \quad 2\theta = \frac{\pi}{6} + 2\pi n \text{ or } \frac{5\pi}{6} + 2\pi n.$$

for $n = 0, 1, -1, 2, -2, \ldots$. It follows that

$$\theta = \frac{\pi}{12} + \pi n \quad \text{or} \quad \frac{5\pi}{12} + \pi n$$

for $n = 0, 1, -1, 2, -2, \ldots$.

Due to symmetry, the total area is double the area between $\theta = \pi/12$ and $\theta = 5\pi/12$. Hence, it is

$$\frac{2}{2} \int_{\pi/12}^{5\pi/12} 4\sin 2\theta - 2 \, d\theta = -2\cos 2\theta - 2\theta \Big|_{\pi/12}^{5\pi/12}$$

$$= -2\cos\frac{5\pi}{6} - \frac{5\pi}{6} + 2\cos\frac{\pi}{6} + \frac{\pi}{6}$$

$$= -2\left(-\frac{\sqrt{3}}{2}\right) - \frac{5\pi}{6} + 2\left(\frac{\sqrt{3}}{2}\right) + \frac{\pi}{6}$$

$$= 2\sqrt{3} - \frac{2\pi}{3}.$$

Fill in (B)! See the glossary for a list of *sine and cosine values in quadrant I*. ∎

Solution 20. ───

We can solve this problem by use of *integration properties*. In particular, note that for x in the interval $[a, b]$, we have

$$f(x) \geq g(x) \quad \text{implies} \quad \int_a^b f(x)\,dx \geq \int_a^b g(x)\,dx.$$

So,

$$f'(x) \geq x \quad \text{implies} \quad \int_x^3 f'(t)\,dt \geq \int_x^3 t\,dt.$$

Because $f(3) = 7$, the *Fundamental theorem of Calculus* tells us

$$\int_x^3 f'(x)\,dt = f(3) - f(x) = 7 - f(x).$$

Furthermore,

$$\int_x^3 t\,dt = \frac{t^2}{2}\bigg|_x^3 = \frac{9}{2} - \frac{x^2}{2}.$$

Hence,

$$7 - f(x) \geq \frac{9}{2} - \frac{x^2}{2} \quad \text{implies} \quad \frac{5}{2} + \frac{x^2}{2} \geq f(x) \quad \text{implies} \quad \int_0^3 \frac{5}{2} + \frac{x^2}{2}\,dx \geq \int_0^3 f(x)\,dx.$$

Since

$$\int_0^3 \frac{5}{2} + \frac{x^2}{2}\,dx = \frac{5}{2}x + \frac{x^3}{6}\bigg|_0^3 = 12,$$

we conclude

$$\int_0^3 f(x)\,dx \leq 12.$$

The answer must be (C). ∎

Solution 21. ───

Option I is true. The map $f : (0, 1) \to (0, 1]$ such that

$$f(x) := \begin{cases} \dfrac{1}{n-1}, & \text{if } x = \dfrac{1}{n} \text{ for } n \in \mathbb{N} \\ x, & \text{otherwise} \end{cases}$$

is one-to-one and onto.

Option II is correct because the image of f could be compact. For example, if $f(x) := 1/2$, then its image is the compact set $\{1/2\}$.

Option III is false. If f were continuous, one-to-one, and onto, there would have to be some value x_1 in the interval $(0, 1)$ such that $f(x_1) = 1$. It would follow that f is increasing on some interval (a, x_1) and decreasing on some interval (x_1, b), where

$$0 < a < x_1 < b < 1.$$

However, this is a contradiction of the one-to-one assumption.

Answer (C) is correct. Mark it and move on! ∎

Solution 22.

Let us compute our integral:

$$\int_{-\infty}^{\infty} xf(x)\,dx = \int_{-1}^{2} \frac{2x|x|}{5}\,dx$$

$$= \int_{-1}^{0} -\frac{2x^2}{5}\,dx + \int_{0}^{2} \frac{2x^2}{5}\,dx$$

$$= -\frac{2x^3}{15}\bigg|_{-1}^{0} + \frac{2x^3}{15}\bigg|_{0}^{2}$$

$$= -\frac{2}{15} + \frac{16}{15}$$

$$= \frac{14}{15}.$$

The answer is (A). ■

Solution 23.

Due to the *Fundamental theorem of finitely generated abelian groups*, there are two abelian groups of order 4. They are $\mathbb{Z}_4$ and $\mathbb{Z}_2 \times \mathbb{Z}_2$. The same theorem tells us that the others have more or fewer abelian groups, e.g. there is only one abelian group of order 7, specifically $\mathbb{Z}_7$, and there are three abelian groups of order 8, specifically $\mathbb{Z}_8$, $\mathbb{Z}_2 \times \mathbb{Z}_4$, and $\mathbb{Z}_2 \times \mathbb{Z}_2 \times \mathbb{Z}_2$. We select (A). ■

Solution 24.

We know $25\pi \approx 25(3.14) = 78.5$. By applying the property $f(1+x) = f(x)$ a total of n times, we see that $f(n+x) = f(x)$ for every positive integer n. Therefore, $f(78+0.5) = f(0.5)$. Since π is a little bigger than 3.14, the value $f'(25\pi)$ is the slope of the segment whose endpoints are $(1/2, 1/2)$ and $(3/4, 1)$. It follows that

$$f'(25\pi) = \frac{1 - 1/2}{3/4 - 1/2} = 2.$$

We conclude that the answer is (D). ■

Solution 25.

Since the sequence $\{x_n\}_{n=1}^{\infty}$ converges, say to x, we have

$$\lim_{n\to\infty} x_{n+1} - \sqrt{15 - 2x_n} = 0 \quad \text{implies} \quad x - \sqrt{15 - 2x} = 0$$

It follows that

$$\begin{aligned}
x &= \sqrt{15 - 2x} \\
\Rightarrow \qquad x^2 &= 15 - 2x \\
\Rightarrow \qquad x^2 + 2x - 15 &= 0 \\
\Rightarrow \qquad (x+5)(x-3) &= 0.
\end{aligned}$$

This means $x = -5$ or $x = 3$. Because the range of the square-root function is the set of nonnegative values, $x = -5$ is an extraneous solution. The correct answer must be 3, so we select (D). ■

58

Solution 26. ———

The *inverse function theorem* theorem from Calculus tells us that

$$(g' \circ f)(x) = \frac{1}{f'(x)}.$$

Since $f(2) = 0$, we know $g(0) = 2$. It follows that $(g' \circ g)(0) = g'(2)$. Then

$$f(6) = 2 \quad \text{implies} \quad (g' \circ g)(0) = (g' \circ f)(6) = \frac{1}{f'(6)} = \frac{1}{3}.$$

The answer must be (C). ■

Solution 27. ———

The equation of the circle is

$$x^2 + (y - k)^2 = 1$$

for some k.

At the points of tangency, the circle and $y = x^2$ have the same slope. Let us compute each derivative. We will differentiate the circle equation using implicit differentiation. This yields

$$2x + 2(y - k)y' = 0 \quad \text{implies} \quad y' = -\frac{x}{y - k}.$$

Since the derivative of $y = x^2$ is $y' = 2x$, at the point of tangency,

$$2x = -\frac{x}{y - k} \quad \text{implies} \quad y - k = -\frac{1}{2}.$$

From our knowledge of the unit circle, we conclude that the points of intersection are

$$\left(-\frac{\sqrt{3}}{2}, k - \frac{1}{2}\right) \quad \text{and} \quad \left(\frac{\sqrt{3}}{2}, k - \frac{1}{2}\right).$$

Because the point of tangency lies on $y = x^2$,

$$k - \frac{1}{2} = \left(\frac{\sqrt{3}}{2}\right)^2 \quad \text{implies} \quad k = \frac{5}{4}.$$

Solving $x^2 + (y - 5/4)^2 = 1$ for y yields

$$y = \frac{5}{4} \pm \sqrt{1 - x^2}.$$

Since we are only concerned with the bottom half of the circle, we need only consider $y = 5/4 - \sqrt{1 - x^2}$. Hence, we just need to evaluate

$$\int_{-\sqrt{3}/2}^{\sqrt{3}/2} \frac{5}{4} - \sqrt{1 - x^2} - x^2 \, dx = 2\int_{0}^{\sqrt{3}/2} \frac{5}{4} - \sqrt{1 - x^2} - x^2 \, dx = 2\int_{0}^{\sqrt{3}/2} \frac{5}{4} - x^2 \, dx - 2\int_{0}^{\sqrt{3}/2} \sqrt{1 - x^2} \, dx$$

Let us consider the two integrals separately. First,

$$2\int_{0}^{\sqrt{3}/2} \frac{5}{4} - x^2 \, dx = 2\left[\frac{5}{4}x - \frac{x^3}{3}\right]_{0}^{\sqrt{3}/2} = 2\left(\frac{5\sqrt{3}}{8} - \frac{\sqrt{3}}{8} - 0\right) = \sqrt{3}.$$

59

We need to use a trigonometric substitution for the other integral. Let $x = \sin\theta$. Then $dx = \cos\theta\,d\theta$. So,

$$2\int_0^{\sqrt{3}/2}\sqrt{1-x^2}\,dx = 2\int_{x=0}^{\sqrt{3}/2}\sqrt{1-\sin^2\theta}\,\cos\theta\,d\theta = 2\int_{\theta=0}^{\pi/3}\cos^2\theta\,d\theta.$$

One of the *power reduction identities* tells us

$$\cos^2\theta = \frac{1}{2}\left(1+\cos 2\theta\right).$$

It follows that

$$2\int_{\theta=0}^{\pi/3}\cos^2\theta\,d\theta = \int_0^{\pi/3} 1 + \cos 2\theta\,d\theta = \left[\theta + \frac{1}{2}\sin 2\theta\right]_0^{\pi/3} = \frac{\pi}{3} + \frac{\sqrt{3}}{4}.$$

Therefore,

$$\int_{-\sqrt{3}/2}^{\sqrt{3}/2}\frac{5}{4} - \sqrt{1-x^2} - x^2\,dx = \sqrt{3} - \left(\frac{\pi}{3} + \frac{\sqrt{3}}{4}\right) = \frac{3\sqrt{3}}{4} - \frac{\pi}{3}.$$

This is option (C). This problem can also be done using only

$$\int_{-\sqrt{3}/2}^{\sqrt{3}/2}x^2\,dx = \frac{\sqrt{3}}{4}$$

and some trigonometry. We have had bad luck with this approach so we opted to solve the problem using more Calculus. ∎

Solution 28. ───

For parametric equations $x = f(t)$ and $y = g(t)$, the arc length from $t = a$ to $t = b$ is

$$\int_a^b \sqrt{\left(\frac{dx}{dt}\right)^2 + \left(\frac{dy}{dt}\right)^2}\,dt.$$

Let us find the pieces:

$$x = 8e^{t/2}\quad\text{implies}\quad\frac{dx}{dt} = 4e^{t/2}\quad\text{and}\quad y = e^t - 4t\quad\text{implies}\quad\frac{dy}{dt} = e^t - 4.$$

If $x = 8$ and $y = 1$, then $t = 0$. If $x = 8e$ and $y = e^2 - 8$, then $t = 2$. Hence, the arc length is

$$\int_0^2 \sqrt{\left(4e^{t/2}\right)^2 + \left(e^t - 4\right)^2}\,dt = \int_0^2 \sqrt{16e^t + e^{2t} - 8e^t + 16}\,dt$$

$$= \int_0^2 \sqrt{e^{2t} + 8e^t + 16}\,dt$$

$$= \int_0^2 \sqrt{(e^t + 4)^2}\,dt$$

$$= \int_0^2 e^t + 4\,dt$$

$$= e^t + 4t\Big|_0^2$$

$$= e^2 + 7.$$

Select answer (E) and move on! ∎

x y $10 - x - y$

Solution 29. ——

Suppose the length of the segment farthest to the left is x and the length of the middle segment is y. Then the length of the right segment is $10 - x - y$. Under this formulation, the sample space is

$$\{(x,y) \in \mathbb{R}^2 : x + y < 10, \ x, y > 0\}.$$

The three segments can be bent into a triangle if and only if the triangle inequality holds. As a result, we have that

$$
\begin{aligned}
x + y &> 10 - x - y & \implies & \quad x + y &> 5 \\
x + (10 - x - y) &> y & \implies & \quad 5 &> y \\
y + (10 - x - y) &> x & \implies & \quad 5 &> x.
\end{aligned}
$$

Let us graph this situation.

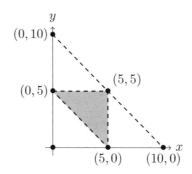

From here, it is clear the area of the sample space is $10(10)/2 = 50$ and the area of the event that the sides of the segment could be bent to form a triangle is $5(5)/2 = 25/2$. Hence, the probability that the event occurs is

$$\frac{25/2}{50} = \frac{1}{4},$$

which is 25%. The answer is (C). ■

Solution 30. ——

This is simply a combination problem. How many ways are there to choose pairs of two vertices, where the order in which we choose the two vertices is irrelevant? The answer is

$$_{10}C_2 = \frac{10!}{2!8!} = 45.$$

It is time to pick (D). ■

Solution 31.

The dimension of

$$P = \{a_0 + a_1 x + a_2 x^2 + \ldots + a_7 x^7 : a_i \in \mathbb{Z}_5\}$$

is 8. Furthermore, notice that D sends terms of the form $a_0 + a_5 x^5$ to zero. As a result, the null space of D is $\{a_0 + a_5 x^5 : a_i \in \mathbb{Z}_5\}$, which has dimension $n = 2$. Due to the *rank nullity theorem*, the rank must be $r = 8 - 2 = 6$. Therefore, (D) is correct. ∎

Solution 32.

Let us go through the steps when `a` = 20 and `b` = 28. Since `a` < `b`, the algorithm sets `max` = 28 and `min` = 20. Then it enters the while loop. Within the first iteration of the while loop it gives `r` = 8, and a new `max` of 20 and a new `min` of 8. For the next iteration, it gives `max` = 8 and `min` = 4. And in the next iteration it gives `max` = 4 and `min` = 0. This is where the while loop terminates, since `min` = 0 is not greater than 0. Hence, the algorithm prints 20*28/4 = 140. This result corresponds to option (D). ∎

Solution 33.

Because $\varphi(k_0)$ is true, so is $\varphi(k_0 + 1)$. If $\varphi(k_0 + 1)$ is true, so is $\varphi(k_0 + 2)$, which implies $\varphi(k_0 + 3)$ is true too, etc. It follows that $\varphi(k)$ is true for $k \geq k_0$. We have no knowledge as to whether $\varphi(k_0 - 1)$ is true or false. Hence, (E) is the correct answer. ∎

Solution 34.

The function f is called the "topologist's sine curve". It is a famous counterexample to the notion that *connectedness* implies *path connectedness*. We will continue as though we do not know this.

Option I is true. It is clear that the sets

$$I_+ = \{(x, f(x)) \in \mathbb{R}^2 : 0 < x \leq 1\} \quad \text{and} \quad I_- = \{(x, f(x)) \in \mathbb{R}^2 : -1 \leq x < 0\}$$

are both connected, so the only point that could be an issue is $(0, 0)$. However,

$$\overline{I}_+ = I_+ \cup \left(\{0\} \times [-1, 1]\right) \quad \text{and} \quad \overline{I}_- = I_- \cup \left(\{0\} \times [-1, 1]\right),$$

both contain $(0, 0)$, so it would be impossible to write $I = A \cup B$ where A and B are nonempty and $\overline{A} \cap B = A \cap \overline{B} = \varnothing$.

Option II is false. Since $\lim_{x \to 0} \sin(1/x)$ does not exist, I is not the graph of a continuous function, so it is not path connected.

Option III is not valid either. Because $\overline{I} = I \cup \left(\{0\} \times [-1, 1]\right) \neq I$, the set I is not closed. Due to the *Heine-Borel theorem*, it is therefore not compact.

We are ready to make our conclusions. Since only I is true, (A) is the correct answer. ∎

Solution 35.

The value

$$\int_0^x f(t)\, dt$$

is the net signed area between f and the x-axis for $x > 0$, and it is the opposite of the net signed area for $x < 0$. As such, our strategy will be to break the interval $[-4, 3]$ into smaller regions in which we can easily compute the signed area.

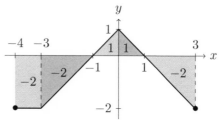

With the picture above in mind, it follows that

$$g(-4) = -(-2 - 2 + 1) = 3, \quad g(-3) = -(-2 + 1) = 1, \quad g(-1) = -1, \quad g(1) = 1$$

and

$$g(3) = 1 + (-2) = -1.$$

From here, it is clear that the absolute maximum is $g(-4)$, so we fill in the bubble for (A). ■

Solution 36.

Option I is true. It is clear

$$-\sqrt{t} \le \sqrt{t} \sin \frac{1}{t} \le \sqrt{t}$$

for t in the interval $(0, 1]$. Note x in I implies x^2 is in $(0, 1]$. Since $-\sqrt{t}$ and $\sqrt{t}$ are bounded over the interval $(0, 1]$, the signed areas under them is also bounded. It follows that the area under $\sqrt{t}\sin(1/t)$ for $0 < t \le 1$ is bounded as well.

Option II is also sound, because f' is bounded. Due to the *Fundamental theorem of Calculus*

$$f'(x) = \frac{d}{dx}\left(\int_0^{x^2} \sqrt{t} \sin \frac{1}{t}\, dt \right) = \sqrt{x^2} \sin\left(\frac{1}{x^2} \right) \cdot 2x = 2x|x| \sin \frac{1}{x^2}.$$

From here, it is clear that $-2 \le f'(x) \le 2$ for x in I.

Option III is false. For $x > 0$, we have

$$f''(x) = 4x \sin \frac{1}{x^2} - \frac{4}{x} \cos \frac{1}{x^2}.$$

Due to the second term of $f''(x)$, the function is unbounded within the interval $(0, 1]$.

Since I and II are true and option III is false, we are ready to conclude that (C) is correct. ■

Solution 37. ——

We say a noninvertible square matrix is "singular". A matrix is noninvertible if and only if its determinant is 0. As a result, we will simply compute the determinant $|A|$, set it equal to 0, and solve for c.

To compute the determinant, we will expand by the first row:

$$\begin{vmatrix} 1 & 0 & -2 \\ c & -9 & -c \\ 0 & c & -1 \end{vmatrix} = 1 \begin{vmatrix} -9 & -c \\ c & -1 \end{vmatrix} - 0 \begin{vmatrix} c & -c \\ 0 & -1 \end{vmatrix} - 2 \begin{vmatrix} c & -9 \\ 0 & c \end{vmatrix} = (9 + c^2) - 2c^2 = 9 - c^2.$$

If $9 - c^2 = 0$, then $c = -3$ or $c = 3$. Therefore, (E) is the answer. ∎

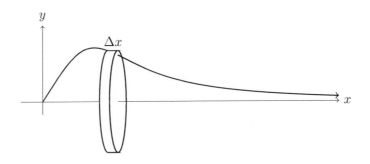

Solution 38. ——

Using the *disk method*, we see that

$$\Delta V = \pi \left(\frac{x}{1 + x^3} \right)^2 \Delta x,$$

where x is in the interval $[0, \infty)$. This implies that the volume

$$V = \pi \int_0^\infty \left(\frac{x}{1 + x^3} \right)^2 dx = \pi \int_0^\infty \frac{x^2}{(1 + x^3)^2} \, dx.$$

A u-substation is a good path forward. Let $u = 1 + x^3$. Then $du = 3x^2 dx$. Hence,

$$V = \frac{\pi}{3} \int_{x=0}^\infty \frac{du}{u^2} \, du = \frac{\pi}{3} \int_{u=1}^\infty \frac{du}{u^2} \, du = \frac{\pi}{3} \left[-\frac{1}{u} \right]_1^\infty = \frac{\pi}{3}.$$

The volume is $\pi/3$, so the answer is (A). ∎

Solution 39. ───

Since $\neg D$ is $|f(x) - f(y)| < \varepsilon$, we see that the statement converts to

$$A\Big(B\left(C \Rightarrow \neg D\right)\Big).$$

Unfortunately, this is not a choice. However, $C \Rightarrow \neg D$ is logically equivalent $\neg C$ or $\neg D$. Let us prove this with a truth table:

C	D	$\neg C$	$\neg D$	$C \Rightarrow \neg D$	$\neg C$ or $\neg D$
T	T	F	F	F	F
T	F	F	T	T	T
F	T	T	F	T	T
F	F	T	T	T	T

Hence, the statement becomes

$$A\Big(B\left(\neg C \text{ or } \neg D\right)\Big).$$

The answer must be (E). ∎

Solution 40. ───

Let us use the *ratio test*:

$$\lim_{n\to\infty} \left| \frac{\dfrac{\Big((n+1)x\Big)^{n+1}}{2\cdot 4\cdot\ldots\cdot 2n\cdot 2(n+1)}}{\dfrac{(nx)^n}{2\cdot 4\cdot\ldots\cdot 2n}} \right| = \lim_{n\to\infty} \left| \frac{\Big((n+1)x\Big)^{n+1}}{2\cdot 4\cdot\ldots\cdot 2n\cdot 2(n+1)} \cdot \frac{2\cdot 4\cdot\ldots\cdot 2n}{(nx)^n} \right|$$

$$= \lim_{n\to\infty} \left| \frac{(n+1)^{n+1}x^{n+1}}{2(n+1)} \cdot \frac{1}{n^n x^n} \right|$$

$$= \lim_{n\to\infty} \frac{(n+1)^n |x|}{2n^n}$$

$$= \lim_{n\to\infty} \left(1 + \frac{1}{n}\right)^n \frac{|x|}{2}$$

$$= \frac{e|x|}{2}.$$

The series converges when $e|x|/2 < 1$. This implies $|x| < 2/e$. So, the radius of convergence is $2/e$. This is (C). ∎

Solution 41. ——

Option I is false. This is equivalent to the claim that every diagonalizable matrix commutes with any matrix of the same dimensions. We can easily disprove this claim with a counterexample. Consider

$$T = \begin{pmatrix} 1 & 0 \\ 0 & -1 \end{pmatrix} \quad \text{and} \quad X = \begin{pmatrix} 1 & 1 \\ 0 & 0 \end{pmatrix}.$$

Clearly, T is diagonalizable using the standard basis of $\mathbb{R}^2$. However,

$$TX = \begin{pmatrix} 1 & 1 \\ 0 & 0 \end{pmatrix} \quad \text{and} \quad XT = \begin{pmatrix} 1 & -1 \\ 0 & 0 \end{pmatrix}.$$

Option II is true. Consider the map $\varphi_T : \mathcal{M}(V) \to \mathcal{M}(V)$ such that $\varphi_T : X \mapsto TX - XT$. The map φ_T is linear. To prove this consider X and Y in $\mathcal{M}(V)$, and α and β in $\mathbb{R}$. Then

$$\begin{aligned} \varphi_T\left(\alpha X + \beta Y\right) &= T\left(\alpha X + \beta Y\right) - \left(\alpha X + \beta Y\right)T \\ &= \alpha TX + \beta TY - \alpha XT - \beta YT \\ &= \alpha\left(TX - XT\right) + \beta\left(TY - YT\right) \\ &= \alpha\varphi_T(X) + \beta\varphi_T(Y). \end{aligned}$$

Furthermore, notice that the null space of φ_T is $\mathcal{U}$ and the range of φ_T is $\mathcal{W}$. Since the dimension of $\mathcal{M}(V)$ is n^2, the *rank nullity theorem* tells us that

$$\dim\left(\mathcal{U}\right) + \dim\left(\mathcal{W}\right) = n^2.$$

Option III is not necessarily true. Indeed, if T is the $n \times n$ identity matrix, then $\dim\left(\mathcal{W}\right) = 0$.

Options I and III are false and II is true. Therefore, (B) is correct. ∎

Solution 42. ——

Lagrange's theorem says that the order of a subgroup must divide the order of the entire group. It follows that (A) and (E) are out because 5 does not divide their orders. If a group has a subgroup of order 2, then the non-identity element of the subgroup must be its own inverse, which means that G cannot have a subgroup of order 2. *Cauchy's group theorem* tells us that a group of even order must have a subgroup of order 2. As a result, (B) and (C) are excluded because those orders are even. By the process of elimination, the answer is (D). Indeed, $\mathbb{Z}_{35}$ has no non-identity element which is its own inverse. ∎

Solution 43. ——

Let us figure out an identity which we can use to simplify the expression. Due to *Euler's formula*, we know $e^{2\pi i} = 1$. This implies $\zeta^5 = 1$. Furthermore,

$$1 - \zeta^5 = 0 \quad \text{implies} \quad (1 - \zeta)(1 + \zeta + \zeta^2 + \zeta^3 + \zeta^4) = 0.$$

Since $\zeta \neq 1$, it follows that

$$1 + \zeta + \zeta^2 + \zeta^3 + \zeta^4 = 0.$$

We are ready to simplify our sum:

$$3 + 3\zeta + 12\zeta^2 + 12\zeta^3 + 12\zeta^4 + 9\zeta^5 + 5\zeta^6$$

$$= 3(1 + \zeta + \zeta^2 + \zeta^3 + \zeta^4) + 9\zeta^2 + 9\zeta^3 + 9\zeta^4 + 9\zeta^5 + 5\zeta^6$$

$$= 3(0) + 9\zeta^2(1 + \zeta + \zeta^2 + \zeta^3 + \zeta^4) - 4\zeta^6$$

$$= 9(0) - 4\zeta^6$$

$$= -4\left(e^{2\pi i/5}\right)^6$$

$$= -4e^{12\pi i/5}$$

$$= -4e^{2\pi i}e^{2\pi i/5}$$

$$= -4e^{2\pi i/5}.$$

This is (A), so select it! ∎

Solution 44.

Option I is true. If the *characteristic polynomial* of an $n \times n$ matrix A is

$$\det(A - \lambda I) = a_n\lambda^n + a_{n-1}\lambda^{n-1} + \ldots + a_1\lambda + a_0,$$

then the *trace* of A is $-a_{n-1}/a_n$. In our case, it follows that the trace of A is $-3/(-1) = 3$.

Option II is valid too. Indeed,

$$\det(A) = \det(A - 0I) = -(0)^3 + 3(0)^2 + 0 - 3 = -3.$$

Option III is false because -3 is not a zero of the characteristic polynomial:

$$-(-3)^3 + 3(-3)^2 + (-3) - 3 = 48.$$

Therefore, (D) is the correct choice. ∎

Solution 45.

Suppose that a solution of the differential equation is of the form $y = e^{mx}$. Then

$$\frac{dy}{dx} = me^{mx} \quad \text{and} \quad \frac{d^2y}{dx^2} = m^2e^{mx}.$$

So,

$$2m^2e^{mx} + 9me^{mx} - 35e^{mx} = 0 \quad \text{implies} \quad 2m^2 + 9m - 35 = 0.$$

Solving yields $m = 5/2$ or $m = -7$.

It follows that $y = e^{-7x}$ and $y = e^{5x/2}$ are solutions. Because any linear combination of the two solutions is also a solution, the general solution is

$$y = C_1e^{-7x} + C_2e^{5x/2},$$

where C_1 and C_2 real numbers. This corresponds to (A). ∎

Solution 46. ―――――――――――――――――――――――――――

The first partial derivatives are

$$f_x(x,y) = 3x^2 + 6xy - 1 \quad \text{and} \quad f_y(x,y) = -3y^2 + 3x^2.$$

Let $f_x(x,y) = 0$ and $f_y(x,y) = 0$. Using the second equation, we have

$$-3y^2 + 3x^2 = 0 \quad \text{implies} \quad y = -x \text{ or } y = x.$$

If $y = x$ and $f_x(x,y) = 0$, then

$$9x^2 - 1 = 0 \quad \text{implies} \quad x = \pm\frac{1}{3}.$$

So, two critical points are $(1/3, 1/3)$ and $(-1/3, -1/3)$.

If $y = -x$ and $f_x(x,y) = 0$, then

$$-3x^2 - 1 = 0 \quad \text{implies} \quad x^2 = -\frac{1}{3}.$$

This is impossible, so this case adds no new critical points.

Since there were no critical points on $y = -x$, all critical points lie on the line $y = x$. This leads us to conclude that (E) is correct.

We are not being timed, so we will use the *second derivatives test* to analyze the critical numbers. The second partial derivatives of f are

$$f_{xx}(x,y) = 6x + 6y, \quad f_{xy}(x,y) = 6x, \quad f_{yx}(x,y) = 6x, \quad \text{and} \quad f_{yy}(x,y) = -6y.$$

So, the Hessian matrix has determinant

$$D = \begin{vmatrix} 6x + 6y & 6x \\ 6x & -6y \end{vmatrix} = -36y(x+y) - 36x^2.$$

We are ready to examine each point:

$\left(\frac{1}{3}, \frac{1}{3}\right)$: $D\big|_{(1/3,1/3)} = -12 < 0$, which means there is a saddle point at $(1/3, 1/3)$.

$\left(-\frac{1}{3}, -\frac{1}{3}\right)$: $D\big|_{(-1/3,-1/3)} = -12 < 0$, which means there is a saddle point at $(-1/3, -1/3)$.

∎

Solution 47. ―――――――――――――――――――――――――――

Notice that $p(x)$ is a second degree Taylor series of $f(x) = \log(x)$ whose center is 1. Furthermore, because the infinite Taylor series for $f(1.1)$ is an alternating series, has terms decreasing in magnitude, and the term of highest degree of $p(1.1)$ is negative, it must be that

$$\log(1.1) - p(1.1) > 0.$$

Taylor's theorem tells us that we can bound the difference by means of the Lagrange error bound:

$$\log(1.1) - p(1.1) \leq \frac{\sup\limits_{z \in I} |f'''(z)|}{3!}(1.1 - 1)^3,$$

where I is the interval with endpoints 1 and 1.1. Since $f'''(x) = 2/x^3$, its supremum over I is $f'''(1) = 2$. Hence, the difference is less than

$$\frac{2}{3!}(1.1 - 1)^3 = \frac{1}{3}(0.1)^3 = \frac{1}{3}(10)^{-3}.$$

This is option (E).   ∎

Solution 48. ──
Our challenge is to find

$$10^{10^{10}} \equiv 3^{10^{10}} \pmod{7}.$$

Due to *Fermat's little theorem*, we know

$$q^{p-1} \equiv 1 \pmod{p},$$

where p and q are co-prime. That means $3^6 \equiv 1 \pmod 7$, which implies $3^{6m} \equiv 1 \pmod 7$ for all integers m. Notice that

$$10^{10} - 4 = 9999999996 = 6\,(\text{some integer})\,.$$

Thus,

$$10^{10^{10}} \equiv 3^{10^{10}} \equiv 3^{10^{10}-4} \cdot 3^4 \equiv 1 \cdot 3^4 \equiv 81 \equiv 4 \pmod 7.$$

We conclude that $10^{10^{10}}$ days from Wednesday will be the same day of the week as four days from Wednesday. Hence, it will be Sunday $10^{10^{10}}$ days from Wednesday. Select (A)!

                                                                                                   ∎

Kate	2
John	2
Kate	2
John	2
Kate	2

John	2
Kate	2
John	2
Kate	2
John	2
Kate	0.5

Solution 49. ──
The tables above show the alternating two-day shifts when Kate and John start, respectively. It is clear Kate's rate is $1/k$ and John's rate is $1/j$. Hence, we have the system

$$\begin{cases} \dfrac{6}{k} + \dfrac{4}{j} = 1 \\[2mm] \dfrac{4.5}{k} + \dfrac{6}{j} = 1. \end{cases}$$

Solving the system shows that $k = 9$ and $j = 12$. To find the number of days it takes the two of them to write a test when they work together, we need to solve the following equation for t:

$$\frac{t}{9} + \frac{t}{12} = 1.$$

The solution is $t = 36/7$ days, which corresponds to (D).   ∎

69

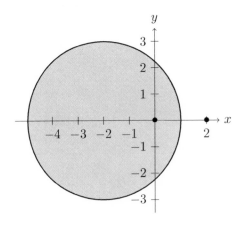

Solution 50.

Due to the *Cauchy's residue theorem*

$$\int_C \frac{dz}{z^3(z-2)} = 2\pi i \operatorname{Res}(f,0) = \frac{2\pi i}{2!} \lim_{z\to 0} \frac{d^2}{dz^2}\left(\frac{1}{z-2}\right) = \pi i \lim_{z\to 0} \frac{2}{(z-2)^3} = -\frac{\pi i}{4}.$$

Select (A). ∎

Solution 51.

The Dihedral group of 8 elements is, by definition, the group of symmetries of a square. There is no reason to believe the symmetries of the four-petaled rose curve are any different. We select (E). ∎

Solution 52.

Option I must be false. If f is continuous, then the image of a compact set is compact. As a result, $f([a,b])$ is compact because $[a,b]$ is compact. Due to the *Heine-Borel theorem*, a subset of $\mathbb{R}$ is closed and bounded if and only if it is compact. This implies $f([a,b])$ is bounded, which contradicts I.

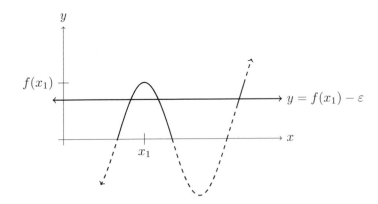

Option II has to be false too. If $f(x) = 0$ has two solutions, then there is a value of x say x_1 where the derivative switches signs. It follows that there is a relative extremum at $x = x_1$. But then option II says there would be another value of x_2 such that $f(x_1) = f(x_2)$. However, this implies that

$$f(x) = f(x_1) - \varepsilon \quad \text{or} \quad f(x) = f(x_1) + \varepsilon$$

70

has three or more solutions for $\varepsilon > 0$ sufficiently small. The graph illustrates the idea when there is a relative maximum at $(x_1, f(x_1))$, which would require $f(x) = f(x_1) - \varepsilon$ to have at least three solutions for $\varepsilon > 0$ small enough.

Option III is out because it is true. We know

$$\lim_{x \to \infty} \frac{f(x)}{x} = \infty \quad \text{implies} \quad \lim_{x \to \infty} f'(x) = \infty$$

is true because it follows from *L'Hôspital's rule*. Let us consider the other direction. Suppose $\lim_{x \to \infty} f'(x) = \infty$. Due to the *Mean value theorem*, there exists an x_n in the interval $(n, 2n)$ such that

$$\frac{f(2n) - f(n)}{n} = f'(x_n) \quad \text{implies} \quad f(2n) = nf'(x_n) + f(n).$$

It follows that

$$\lim_{x \to \infty} \frac{f(x)}{x} = \lim_{n \to \infty} \frac{f(2n)}{2n} = \lim_{n \to \infty} \frac{nf'(x_n) + f(n)}{2n} = \frac{1}{2} \lim_{n \to \infty} f'(x_n) + \frac{f(n)}{n}.$$

Because $f'(x_n) \to \infty$ as $n \to \infty$, either the last limit must go to ∞ or $f(n)/n$ goes to $-\infty$. The latter scenario is impossible because $f(n)$ is increasing for n sufficiently large due to the fact that $f'(n) \to \infty$ as $n \to \infty$.

Since I and II are in and III is out, the answer is (D). ∎

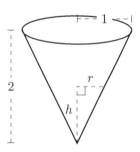

Solution 53. ――――――――――――――――――――――――――――――――――――――

This is a classic related rates problem. We know $dV/dt = -3$ and we want to find $dh/dt\big|_{h=3/2}$. Because r and h are proportional

$$\frac{r}{h} = \frac{1}{2} \quad \text{implies} \quad r = \frac{h}{2} \quad \text{implies} \quad V = \frac{\pi}{3}\left(\frac{h}{2}\right)^2 h = \frac{\pi}{12}h^3.$$

It follows that

$$\frac{dV}{dt} = \frac{\pi}{4}h^2 \frac{dh}{dt} \quad \text{implies} \quad -3 = \frac{\pi}{4}\left(\frac{3}{2}\right)^2 \frac{dh}{dt}\bigg|_{h=3/2} \quad \text{implies} \quad \frac{dh}{dt}\bigg|_{h=3/2} = -\frac{16}{3\pi}.$$

The answer is (E). ∎

Solution 54. ───

The *necessary and sufficient* condition for a function to be analytic is that for

$$f(x + iy) = u(x, y) + iv(x, y),$$

we have

$$\frac{\partial u}{\partial x} = \frac{\partial v}{\partial y} \quad \text{and} \quad \frac{\partial u}{\partial y} = -\frac{\partial v}{\partial x}.$$

So,

$$g_x(x, y) = e^y \sin x \quad \text{and} \quad g_y(x, y) = -e^y \cos x.$$

We can use "partial integration" to find $g(x, y)$:

$$g(x, y) = \int e^y \sin x \; dx = -e^y \cos x + h_1(y) \quad \text{and} \quad g(x, y) = \int -e^y \cos x \; dy = -e^y \cos x + h_2(x).$$

The functions h_1 and h_2 are functions of y and x, respectively, because in "partial integration" we consider the variable we are not integrating with respect to a constant.

By inspection of our two equations for g, we see

$$g(x, y) = -e^y \cos x + C$$

for some real number C. It follows that

$$g\left(\frac{\pi}{2}, 7\right) - g(0, 0) = -e^7 \cos \frac{\pi}{2} + e^0 \cos 0 = 1.$$

We conclude that (C) is correct. ∎

Solution 55. ───

Option I is false. Consider

$$A = \begin{pmatrix} 0 & -1 \\ 1 & 0 \end{pmatrix}.$$

Denote the *trace* of A^2 by $\text{tr}(A^2)$. Then

$$A^2 = \begin{pmatrix} -1 & 0 \\ 0 & -1 \end{pmatrix} \quad \text{implies} \quad \text{tr}\left(A^2\right) = -2.$$

Option II is sound. Consider an arbitrary vector $\mathbf{v}$. Then

$$\mathbf{v} = A\mathbf{v} + (\mathbf{v} - A\mathbf{v}).$$

If $A^2\mathbf{v} = A\mathbf{v}$, this means that we can deconstruct any vector $\mathbf{v}$ into the sum of a vector invariant under A and a vector which is sent to the null space of A. It follows that there is a basis for A which contains only eigenvectors with eigenvalues of 1 or 0. So, the trace must be nonnegative.

Option III is false. Consider the 2×2 matrices $A = I$ and $B = I$:

$$\text{tr}(A) = 2, \quad \text{tr}(B) = 2, \quad \text{and} \quad \text{tr}(AB) = 2.$$

We conclude that only II is correct. Select (A) and move on. ∎

Solution 56. ——

After a bit of thought, it is clear that the random variable

$$X = X_1 + X_2 + \ldots + X_{100}$$

has a *binomial distribution*. As a result, its respective mean, variance, and standard deviation are

$$\mu = 100\left(\frac{1}{2}\right) = 50, \quad \text{Var}(X) = 100\left(\frac{1}{2}\right)\left(\frac{1}{2}\right) = 25, \quad \text{and} \quad \sigma = \sqrt{25} = 5.$$

Let us go through our choices:

(A) $\text{Var}(X){=}25$

(B) This is the probability that X is more than five standard deviations from the mean. It is highly unlikely for an outcome to be so far from the mean, so (B) is about 0.

(C) The mean of our binomial distribution is by definition

$$\sum_{k=0}^{100} k\binom{100}{k}\left(\frac{1}{2}\right)^k\left(\frac{1}{2}\right)^{100-k}.$$

We know the mean of our distribution is 50. Furthermore, since

$$k\binom{100}{k}\left(\frac{1}{2}\right)^k \geq k\binom{100}{k}\left(\frac{1}{2}\right)^k\left(\frac{1}{2}\right)^{100-k}$$

for $k = 0, 1, \ldots, 100$, it follows that

$$\sum_{k=0}^{100} k\binom{100}{k}\left(\frac{1}{2}\right)^k \geq \sum_{k=0}^{100} k\binom{100}{k}\left(\frac{1}{2}\right)^k\left(\frac{1}{2}\right)^{100-k} = 50.$$

(D) Since the probability $X \leq \mu$ is equal to the probability that $X \geq \mu$, we know $100P(X \geq 60)$ is less than 50. Indeed, we can use the *empirical rule* to conclude that $100P(X \geq 60) \approx 2.5$.

(D) 30 is smaller than 50.

Hence, the answer must be (C) ■

Solution 57. ——

Our first task is to rewrite the sum using summation notation:

$$\lim_{n\to\infty} \frac{1}{n} + \frac{1}{2+n} + \frac{1}{4+n} + \ldots + \frac{1}{3n} = \lim_{n\to\infty} \sum_{k=0}^{n} \frac{1}{2k+n}.$$

It is easier to convert this limit of the sum into an integral and then evaluate. As a result, we will think of the sum as a Riemann sum. Recall that for f a continuous function on the closed interval $[a, b]$, we have

$$\lim_{n\to\infty} \sum_{k=1}^{n} f(x_k)\Delta x = \int_a^b f(x)\,dx,$$

where

$$x_k = a + k \cdot \Delta x \quad \text{and} \quad \Delta x = \frac{b-a}{n}.$$

73

Let us rewrite our sum a bit more to reformulate it as a Riemann sum:

$$\lim_{n\to\infty}\sum_{k=0}^{n}\frac{1}{2k+n} = \lim_{n\to\infty}\frac{1}{n}+\sum_{k=1}^{n}\frac{1}{1+2k/n}\cdot\frac{1}{n}$$

$$= 0 + \lim_{n\to\infty}\sum_{k=1}^{n}\frac{1}{2}\cdot\frac{1}{1+2k/n}\cdot\frac{2}{n}$$

$$= \frac{1}{2}\lim_{n\to\infty}\sum_{k=1}^{n}\frac{1}{1+2k/n}\cdot\frac{2}{n}$$

Let

$$f(x):=\frac{1}{x},\quad x_k:=1+\frac{2k}{n},\quad\text{and}\quad \Delta x:=\frac{2}{n}.$$

It follows that $a=1$. Since our Δx implies that the length of the interval is 2, we see that $b=3$. Hence,

$$\frac{1}{2}\lim_{n\to\infty}\sum_{k=1}^{n}\frac{1}{1+2k/n}\cdot\frac{2}{n} = \frac{1}{2}\int_{1}^{3}\frac{1}{x}\,dx = \frac{1}{2}\log x\Big|_{1}^{3} = \frac{1}{2}\log 3 - 0 = \log\sqrt{3}.$$

The answer is (C). A list *logarithm properties* is located in the glossary. ∎

Solution 58. ───

Option I is false. A subset of $\mathbb{R}$ must be both closed and bounded for it to be compact, due to the *Heine-Borel theorem*. As a counterexample to our situation, consider the closed set $[0,\infty)$. Clearly, the open cover

$$\{(-1,n)\subseteq\mathbb{R}:n=1,2,3,\ldots\}$$

has no finite subcover.

Option II is valid. What is described is sequential compactness, which is equivalent to compactness in $\mathbb{R}$. Indeed, A must be closed and bounded if each sequence has a convergent subsequence. If A were not bounded then for each n we could pick an x_n in A such that $|x_n|>n$, and no subsequence of $\{x_n\}_{n=1}^{\infty}$ would converge. If A were not closed, then it would not contain a limit point of A, say y, and for each n we would pick a y_n in the intersection of A and the ball of center y and radius $1/n$; all subsequences of $\{y_n\}_{n=1}^{\infty}$ would converge to y.

Option III is false. Consider $A_k=\{1/k\}$. We see

$$B=\left\{1,\ \frac{1}{2},\ \frac{1}{3},\ldots\right\}.$$

It is clear that 0 is in $\overline{B}$. However, $\overline{A_k}=\{1/k\}$, which implies

$$\bigcup_{k=1}^{\infty}\overline{A_k}=B.$$

Since B does not contain 0, we have $\overline{B}\neq B$.

We conclude that only II is true. Fill in the bubble for (B). ∎

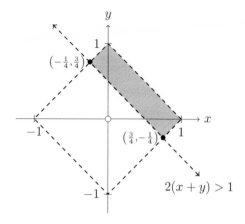

Solution 59. ———

Drawing a picture, we see that the sample space is the interior of a square with a hole in the center. The vertices of the square are $(1,0)$, $(0,1)$, $(-1,0)$, and $(0,-1)$. A little math shows that the area of the sample space is 2 because the sides have length $\sqrt{2}$.

The event $2(x+y) > 1$ forms a rectangle within the sample space. Two of its vertices are $(1,0)$ and $(0,1)$. The other two can be found by solving the systems

$$\begin{cases} 2(x+y) &= 1 \\ -x + y &= 1 \end{cases} \quad \text{and} \quad \begin{cases} 2(x+y) &= 1 \\ -x + y &= -1. \end{cases}$$

Their solutions are $(-1/4, 3/4)$ and $(3/4, -1/4)$, respectively. Using the distance formula, we see that the sides of the rectangle have lengths $\sqrt{2}/4$ and $\sqrt{2}$. Hence, the area within the sample space where $2(x+y) > 1$ is $1/2$

We conclude that the probability of $2(x+y) > 1$ within our sample space is

$$\frac{1/2}{2} = \frac{1}{4}.$$

Select (B) and move on. ■

Solution 60. ───────────────────────────────────────

The *work* done by a vector field $\mathbf{F}$ when an object moves along a smooth path C which is described by $\mathbf{r}(t)$, where t goes from a to b is

$$W = \int_C \mathbf{F} \cdot d\mathbf{r} = \int_a^b \mathbf{F}\left(\mathbf{r}(t)\right) \cdot \mathbf{r}'(t) \; dt.$$

Therefore, the work done by $\mathbf{F}$ is

$$
\begin{aligned}
W &= \int_0^{\pi/2} \left\langle \sin t, -\cos t, \frac{3}{\pi} \right\rangle \cdot \langle -\sin t, \cos t, 2t \rangle \; dt \\
&= \int_0^{\pi/2} -\sin^2 t - \cos^2 t + \frac{6}{\pi} t \; dt \\
&= \int_0^{\pi/2} -1 + \frac{6}{\pi} t \; dt \\
&= -t + \frac{3}{\pi} t^2 \Big|_0^{\pi/2} \\
&= \frac{\pi}{4}.
\end{aligned}
$$

This is (D)! ∎

Solution 61. ───────────────────────────────────────

Let us perform the calculations. There are

$$\binom{25}{3} = \frac{25!}{3!22!} = 2300$$

ways to choose 3 of the 25 suitcases. The respective numbers of ways to choose 2 of the 5 damaged and 1 of the 20 undamaged suitcases are

$$\binom{5}{2} = \frac{5!}{2!3!} = 10 \quad \text{and} \quad \binom{20}{1} = \frac{20!}{1!19!} = 20.$$

Hence, the probability of choosing 2 damaged and 1 undamaged suitcase is

$$\frac{10 \cdot 20}{2300} = \frac{2}{23}.$$

This corresponds to choice (C). ∎

Solution 62. ───────────────────────────────────────

Suppose the interior of C is D. Since the area of D is 2, *Green's theorem* tells us

$$\oint_C x \sin x^2 \; dx + (3e^{y^2} - 2x) \; dy = \iint_D -2 - 0 \; dA = -2\,(2) = -4.$$

Pick option (A). ∎

Solution 63. ───

We want to minimize $\sqrt{x^2 + y^2 + z^2}$ subject to the constraint $3x - 2y + z = 4$. Since the square root is monotonic, the expression $\sqrt{x^2 + y^2 + z^2}$ is minimized at the same point as $f(x, y, z) := x^2 + y^2 + z^2$.

Therefore, our task is the following optimization problem:

$$\begin{aligned} \text{minimum} \quad & f(x, y, z) = x^2 + y^2 + z^2 \\ \text{subject to} \quad & 3x - 2y + z = 4 \end{aligned}$$

Using the *method of Lagrange multipliers*, we see

$$2x = 3\lambda, \quad 2y = -2\lambda, \quad \text{and} \quad 2z = \lambda.$$

It follows that

$$x = 3z \quad \text{and} \quad y = -2z.$$

We have

$$g(3z, -2z, z) = 4 \quad \text{implies} \quad z = \frac{2}{7}.$$

So, the only extreme value is $(6/7, -4/7, 2/7)$. Because there is a minimum distance from the origin, this must be the point which produces that result. We conclude that (E) is correct. ∎

Solution 64. ───

Option I is true. Indeed,

$$\lim_{n \to \infty} \frac{nx}{1 + nx^2} = f(x) = \begin{cases} \dfrac{1}{x}, & \text{if } 0 < x \leq 1 \\[2mm] 0, & \text{if } x = 0. \end{cases}$$

Option II is unsound. The function f_n is continuous for each n and the *uniform convergence theorem* tells us that f would have to be continuous if the sequence were to converge uniformly. Since f is not continuous, $\{f_n\}_{n=1}^{\infty}$ does not converge uniformly.

Option III is false. We have

$$\int_0^1 f_n(x) \, dx = \int_0^1 \frac{nx}{1 + nx^2} = \frac{1}{2} \log(1 + nx^2) \Big|_0^1 = \frac{1}{2} \log(1 + n)$$

and

$$\int_{1/n}^1 \lim_{n \to \infty} f_n(x) \, dx = \int_{1/n}^1 \frac{1}{x} \, dx = \log x \Big|_{1/n}^1 = \log n.$$

It follows that

$$\left| \int_0^1 f_n(x) \, dx - \int_{1/n}^1 \lim_{n \to \infty} f_n(x) \, dx \right| = \left| \frac{1}{2} \log(1 + n) - \log n \right| = \left| \log \sqrt{1 + n} - \log n \right| = \left| \log \frac{\sqrt{1 + n}}{n} \right|.$$

As $n \to \infty$,

$$\frac{\sqrt{1 + n}}{n} \to 0 \quad \text{implies} \quad \left| \log \frac{\sqrt{1 + n}}{n} \right| \to \infty.$$

Since only I was correct, we select (A). A list of *logarithm properties* is located in the glossary. ∎

Solution 65.

The outermost gray area is

$$1 - \pi \left(\frac{1}{2}\right)^2 = 1 - \frac{\pi}{4}.$$

The second largest square and circle are similar to the largest square and circle. The scale factor from the larger to the smaller is $1/\sqrt{2}$. This implies the scale factor between their areas is $\left(1/\sqrt{2}\right)^2 = 1/2$. Indeed, the scale factor between any two consecutive areas is $1/2$. It follows that the total gray area is

$$\sum_{k=1}^{\infty} \left(1 - \frac{\pi}{4}\right)\left(\frac{1}{2}\right)^{k-1} = \left(1 - \frac{\pi}{4}\right) \cdot \frac{1}{1 - 1/2} = 2 - \frac{\pi}{2}.$$

This is (C), so choose it. ∎

Solution 66.

Option I is not a *ring*. It is clear $\sqrt[3]{4}$ is in the set, but

$$\left(\sqrt[3]{4}\right)\left(\sqrt[3]{4}\right) = \sqrt[3]{16} = 2\sqrt[3]{2}$$

is not, which means that the set is not closed under multiplication.

Option II is also not a ring. Indeed, the distributive property does not hold. Consider

$$f(x) = x^2, \quad g(x) = 1, \quad \text{and} \quad h(x) = 2.$$

Then

$$\left(f \circ (g + h)\right)(x) = (1 + 2)^2 = 9 \quad \text{and} \quad \left(f \circ g + f \circ h\right)(x) = 1^2 + 2^2 = 5.$$

Option III is the infamous quaternions. They form a ring.

Because options I and II are not rings and option III is, the correct answer must be (B). Select it and take a break! ∎

Chapter 5

Practice Test 2 Solutions

Solution 1. ───

We will use similar triangles. Note that triangle ADE is similar to triangle ACF. Suppose $AG = FG = x$ and $DE = y$. Then $EF = 2x$. It follows that $AE = 4x$ and $AF = 2x$. So, we have

$$\frac{DE}{AE} = \frac{CF}{AF} \quad \text{implies} \quad \frac{y}{4x} = \frac{CF}{2x} \quad \text{implies} \quad CF = \frac{y}{2}.$$

We can now use what we know about trapezoid $CDEF$. In terms of x and y, its area is

$$\frac{2x\,(y + y/2)}{2} = \frac{3xy}{2}.$$

This leads us to

$$\frac{3xy}{2} = 9 \quad \text{implies} \quad xy = 6.$$

We are ready to make our final conclusions. The area of triangle ADE is

$$\frac{4xy}{2} = 2xy = 2(6) = 12.$$

Fill in the bubble for (C) and peel out! ■

Solution 2. ───

The value of

$$\int_{-2}^{1} f(x)\ dx$$

is the net signed area between f and the x-axis for $-2 \le x \le 1$. As a result, our strategy will be to partition the interval $[-2, 1]$ into smaller intervals in which we can easily compute the signed area under the curve.

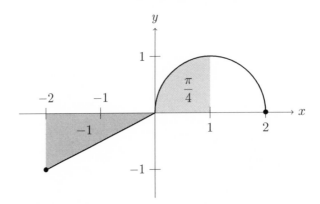

With the picture above in mind, it follows that

$$\int_{-2}^{1} f(x)\ dx = -1 + \frac{\pi}{4} = \frac{\pi - 4}{4}.$$

The answer must be (A). ■

80

Solution 3.

We have

$$\lim_{n\to\infty} e^{-n}\sqrt{e^{n+1}+1} - e^{-(n+1)}\sqrt{e^n+1} = \lim_{n\to\infty} \frac{e\sqrt{e^{n+1}+1} - \sqrt{e^n+1}}{e^{n+1}}$$

$$= \lim_{n\to\infty} \frac{e^{n/2}\left(e\sqrt{e+e^{-n}} - \sqrt{1+e^{-n}}\right)}{e^{n+1}}$$

$$= \lim_{n\to\infty} \frac{e\sqrt{e+e^{-n}} - \sqrt{1+e^{-n}}}{e^{n/2+1}}.$$

From here, we see that

$$e\sqrt{e+e^{-n}} - \sqrt{1+e^{-n}} \longrightarrow e\sqrt{e+0} - \sqrt{1+0} = e^{3/2} - 1$$

and $e^{n/2+1} \to \infty$ as $n \to \infty$. Therefore,

$$\lim_{n\to\infty} e^{-n}\sqrt{e^{n+1}+1} - e^{-(n+1)}\sqrt{e^n+1} = 0.$$

Pick (D) and move on! ■

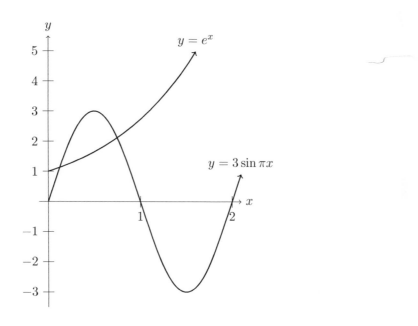

Solution 4.

After drawing a graph, we see that there are two solutions. If you are comfortable graphing, it might be time to select (C) and move on. For those that are not, we will further buttress our conclusion using the *intermediate value theorem.*

We can verify that there are two intersections using the intermediate value theorem. Consider $f(x) := e^x - 3\sin\pi x$. It is clear that f is continuous everywhere and the number of zeros of f is the number of intersections of the two graphs. Let us apply the intermediate value theorem on the intervals $[0, 1/2]$, $[1/2, 1]$, $[1, 2]$, and $[2, \infty)$; this particular choice of intervals is motived by the fact that the period of $y = 3\sin\pi x$ is 2 and the graph of a sine function switches from increasing to decreasing or positive to negative every one-fourth its period.

Consider the interval $[0, 1/2]$. It is clear

$$f(0) = 1 - 0 = 1 > 0 \quad \text{and} \quad f(1/2) = e^{1/2} - 3.$$

Since $e^{1/2} < 4^{1/2} = 2$, we know $f(1/2) < 0$. Therefore, there is at least one zero of f in the interval $[0, 1/2]$. Because $y = e^x$ and $y = \sin 3\pi x$ behave almost linearly over this small interval, we conclude this is the only zero.

Let us take a look at the interval $[1/2, 1]$. We have

$$f(1/2) = e^{1/2} - 3 < 0 \quad \text{and} \quad f(1) = e - \sin \pi = e > 0.$$

Hence, there must be at least one zero in $[1/2, 1]$. Since we know how our two graphs look on a small interval, we can say this is the only intersection in the interval.

On the interval $[1, 2]$, we know $e^x > 0$ and $3 \sin \pi x < 0$, so $f(x) > 0$ for all x in the interval. It follows that there is no intersection within this interval.

For x in the interval $[2, \infty)$, the function f has no zeros. This is because

$$e^x > 2^x \geq 4 \quad \text{and} \quad -3 \leq 3 \sin \pi x \leq 3$$

for all real x, which means

$$f(x) > 4 - 3 = 1 \text{ for } x \geq 2.$$

Thus, there are a total of two intersections. We select (C) and continue! ∎

Solution 5.

This reduces to an equivalent problem with *bases*, since every subspace has a basis and the number of elements in a basis is its dimension. Consider a basis for $U_1 \cap U_2$ and extend it to a basis of U_1. Call the set $\mathcal{B}_1$ the basis for U_1. Extend $\mathcal{B}_1 \cap U_2$ to a basis of U_2, and call it $\mathcal{B}_2$. Extend $\mathcal{B}_1 \cup \mathcal{B}_2$ to a basis of V, and call it $\mathcal{B}$. We need to find what the cardinality of $\mathcal{B}_1 \cap \mathcal{B}_2$ cannot be. Using the *inclusion-exclusion principle* on $\mathcal{B}_1$ and $\mathcal{B}_2$,

$$|\mathcal{B}_1 \cup \mathcal{B}_2| = |\mathcal{B}_1| + |\mathcal{B}_2| - |\mathcal{B}_1 \cap \mathcal{B}_2|.$$

Since $\mathcal{B}_1 \cup \mathcal{B}_2 \subseteq \mathcal{B}$,

$$|\mathcal{B}_1| + |\mathcal{B}_2| - |\mathcal{B}_1 \cap \mathcal{B}_2| \leq |\mathcal{B}|.$$

Because $\dim(U_1) = \dim(U_2) = 5$ and $\dim(V) = 8$, we have

$$5 + 5 - |\mathcal{B}_1 \cap \mathcal{B}_2| \leq 8 \quad \text{implies} \quad |\mathcal{B}_1 \cap \mathcal{B}_2| \geq 2.$$

Therefore, $U_1 \cap U_2$ cannot have dimension 0. We pick (A). ∎

Solution 6.

The most common process to find the equation of a plane, at least in third-semester Calculus, is as follows.

1. Find a vector normal to the plane, usually by means of taking the cross-product of two vectors in the plane.

2. Find a vector whose tail is a known point in the plane and whose tip is an arbitrary point (x, y, z) in the plane.

3. Dot the normal vector in step 1 with the vector in step 2.

4. Since the vectors are orthogonal, set the dot product equal to 0. This furnishes an equation.

We will use these steps to find our plane.

Step 1. We will find two vectors parallel to the plane and cross them to find a normal vector. Since the points $(1, 0, 0)$, $(2, 2, 0)$, and $(1, 0, 1)$ are on the plane, the vectors

$$\langle 2 - 1, 2 - 0, 0 - 0 \rangle = \langle 1, 2, 0 \rangle \quad \text{and} \quad \langle 1 - 1, 0 - 0, 1 - 0 \rangle = \langle 0, 0, 1 \rangle$$

are parallel to the plane. Therefore, the vector

$$\langle 1, 2, 0 \rangle \times \langle 0, 0, 1 \rangle = \begin{vmatrix} \mathbf{i} & \mathbf{j} & \mathbf{k} \\ 1 & 2 & 0 \\ 0 & 0 & 1 \end{vmatrix} = 0 \begin{vmatrix} \mathbf{j} & \mathbf{k} \\ 2 & 0 \end{vmatrix} - 0 \begin{vmatrix} \mathbf{i} & \mathbf{k} \\ 1 & 0 \end{vmatrix} + 1 \begin{vmatrix} \mathbf{i} & \mathbf{j} \\ 1 & 2 \end{vmatrix} = 2\mathbf{i} - \mathbf{j}$$

is normal to the plane. Note that we expanded the determinant by the third row.

Step 2. Consider an arbitrary point (x, y, z) on the plane. Since $(1, 0, 0)$ is contained on the plane, the vector $\langle x - 1, y - 0, z - 0 \rangle = \langle x - 1, y, z \rangle$ lies on the plane.

Step 3. We will take the dot product of our normal vector $\langle 2, -1, 0 \rangle$ and our vector on the plane $\langle x - 1, y, z \rangle$:

$$\langle 2, -1, 0 \rangle \cdot \langle x - 1, y, z \rangle = 2(x - 1) - y.$$

Step 4. Since the vectors $\langle 2, -1, 0 \rangle$ and $\langle x - 1, y, z \rangle$ are orthogonal, their dot product is zero. Hence,

$$2(x - 1) - y = 0 \quad \text{implies} \quad 2x - y = 2.$$

This corresponds to (B). ∎

Solution 7.

An *inflection point*, on the graph of a twice differentiable function, is a point where the second derivative switches signs. As a result, we need to find the second derivative of $f(x) = x^3 - 3x^2 + 5$. Using basic Calculus, we have

$$f'(x) = 3x^2 - 6x \quad \text{and} \quad f''(x) = 6x - 6.$$

From here, it is clear that the second derivative $f''(x) = 6x - 6$ switches from positive to negative at $x = 1$. The y-value of f corresponding to $x = 1$ is

$$f(1) = 1^3 - 3(1)^2 + 5 = 3.$$

It follows that $(1, 3)$ is an inflection point.

It is time to find the tangent line. The slope of the graph at $(1, 3)$ is

$$f'(1) = 3(1)^2 - 6(1) = -3.$$

Therefore, the tangent line is $y = -3x + 6$.

To find the area contained between the x-axis, y-axis, and the equation $y = -3x + 6$, we will draw a graph.

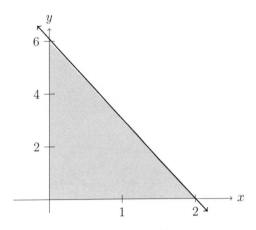

From here, it is clear that the area is $2(6)/2 = 6$. Select (C)! ∎

Solution 8.

We will rewrite f and then see if we can find a pattern. We have

$$f(x) = x(e^{-x} + x) = xe^{-x} + x^2.$$

Let us analyze the derivatives:

$$f'(x) = e^{-x} - xe^{-x} + 2x, \qquad f''(x) = -e^{-x} - e^{-x} + xe^{-x} + 2$$
$$= -2e^{-x} + xe^{-x} + 2,$$

$$f'''(x) = 2e^{-x} + e^{-x} - xe^{-x} \quad \text{and} \quad f^{(4)}(x) = -3e^{-x} - e^{-x} + xe^{-x}$$
$$= 3e^{-x} - xe^{-x}, \qquad\qquad\qquad = -4e^{-x} + xe^{-x}.$$

It looks like, for $n > 2$, the n-th derivative is

$$f^{(n)}(x) = (-1)^{n+1} \left(ne^{-x} - xe^{-x} \right).$$

We conclude that the 100th derivative

$$f^{(100)}(x) = (-1)^{101} \left(100e^{-x} - xe^{-x} \right) = xe^{-x} - 100e^{-x}.$$

Select (A). ∎

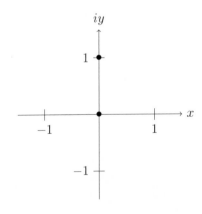

Solution 9.

We will rewrite the relationship. Suppose $z = x + iy$, where x and y are real numbers. Then $|z|^2 = x^2 + y^2$, and

$$\overline{-iz} = \overline{-i(x + iy)} = \overline{y - ix} = y + ix.$$

Therefore,

$$|z|^2 = \overline{-iz} \quad \text{implies} \quad x^2 + y^2 = y + ix.$$

It follows that that $x^2 + y^2 = y$ and $x = 0$. If $x = 0$, then $y^2 = y$, which means $y = 0$ or $y = 1$. Hence, the equation describes two points in the complex domain, 0 and i. Fill in the bubble for (B)! ∎

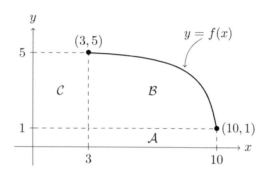

Solution 10.

Consider regions $\mathcal{A}$, $\mathcal{B}$, and $\mathcal{C}$ as shown above. We want to find

$$\int_1^5 f^{-1}(y) \, dy = \text{area}\,(\mathcal{B}) + \text{area}\,(\mathcal{C}).$$

Notice that

$$\int_3^{10} f(x) \, dx = \text{area}\,(\mathcal{A}) + \text{area}\,(\mathcal{B}) = 20.$$

Because $\mathcal{A}$ and $\mathcal{C}$ are rectangles,

$$\text{area}\,(\mathcal{A}) = 7(1) = 7 \quad \text{and} \quad \text{area}\,(\mathcal{C}) = 4(3) = 12.$$

So,

$$7 + \text{area}\,(\mathcal{B}) = 20 \quad \text{implies} \quad \text{area}\,(\mathcal{B}) = 13.$$

Therefore,

$$\int_1^5 f^{-1}(y) \, dy = 13 + 12 = 25.$$

The answer is (D)! ∎

85

Solution 11.

Option I is true. If $\lim_{n\to\infty} a_n/b_n = \infty$ and A converges, then B must converge. This is because $\lim_{n\to\infty} a_n/b_n = \infty$ implies the positive b_n goes to 0 far faster than a_n does. Alternatively, the conclusion follows from the *limit comparison test*.

Option II is false. Suppose

$$a_1 = 1 \quad \text{and} \quad a_n = \frac{1}{n\log n}$$

for $n > 1$. Then

$$\lim_{n\to\infty} na_n = \lim_{n\to\infty} n\left(\frac{1}{n\log n}\right) = \lim_{n\to\infty} \frac{1}{\log n} = 0.$$

However, A diverges in this case. The *integral test* can be used to prove this.

Option III is false. If $a_n = 1/n^2$, then

$$\frac{\sqrt{1/n^2}}{1 + 1/n^2} = \frac{n}{n^2 + 1}.$$

Notice that $\sum n/(n^2 + 1)$ diverges despite the fact that $\sum 1/n^2$ converges

We conclude that only option I is true. As a result, we fill in (A). ∎

Solution 12.

Immediately, we notice that (C) and (D) are mutually exclusive propositions. Therefore, at most one of the two can be correct. As a result, we will restrict our analysis accordingly.

The point $(1, 1)$ is a local minimum. We can prove this using the *second derivative test*. Let us find the second derivative:

$$\frac{dy}{dx} = x^3 - y \quad \text{implies} \quad \frac{d^2y}{dx^2} = 3x^2 - \frac{dy}{dx} = 3x^2 - x^3 + y.$$

So, we have

$$\frac{dy}{dx}\bigg|_{(1,1)} = 1^3 - 1 = 0 \quad \text{and} \quad \frac{d^2y}{dx^2}\bigg|_{(1,1)} = 3(1)^2 - (1)^3 + 1 = 3.$$

Because $dy/dx\big|_{(1,1)} = 0$, we know that $(1, 1)$ is a critical point. Because $d^2y/dx^2\big|_{(1,1)} > 0$, it is a relative minimum.

Since option (C) is true, option (D) must be false. Select it and continue! ∎

Solution 13.

The domain of $g(x) = \log x$ is $x > 0$, which means that the domain of $f(x) = \log(\tan x)$ is the set of values of x such that $\tan x > 0$. From our knowledge of the graph of tangent, the domain of f includes the interval $(0, \pi/2)$ since this is the interval where the principal period of tangent is positive. Because tangent is periodic with period π, we conclude that the domain is

$$\bigcup_{n\in\mathbb{Z}} \left(0 + \pi n, \frac{\pi}{2} + \pi n\right) = \bigcup_{n\in\mathbb{Z}} \left(\pi n, \frac{\pi}{2} + \pi n\right).$$

The answer is (B)! ∎

Solution 14.

The characteristic polynomial of A is

$$p(\lambda) = \begin{vmatrix} 2 - \lambda & -4 \\ -4 & 2 - \lambda \end{vmatrix} = (2 - \lambda)^2 - 16 = \lambda^2 - 4\lambda - 12.$$

The sum of the zeros of p is the sum of the eigenvalues of A. Since the coefficient in front of λ in the polynomial $p(\lambda)$ is the opposite of the sum of the zeros of p, we conclude that the sum of the eigenvalues of A is $-(-4) = 4$. Select (B) and continue! ∎

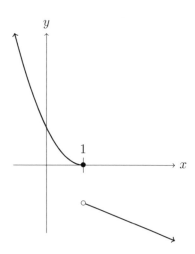

Solution 15.

To be invertible, f must be one-to-one, which pictorially means that the graph of f must pass the horizontal line test. The graph above illustrates an acceptable ray. Note that the graph of $x^2 - 2x + 1 = (x - 1)^2$ for $x \leq 1$ is the left half of a parabola.

After we have drawn a picture, a few key observations become clear. We need $a < 0$, and $a(1) + b = a + b \leq 0$. Only (A) and (B) have $a < 0$. Of those, only (A) satisfies the $a + b < 0$ criterion. So, fill in (A)'s bubble! ∎

Solution 16.

Euclid's algorithm for polynomial division tells us that the remainder when a polynomial is divided by the quadratic $x^2 - 1$ must have degree 1, so the remainder must be of the form $ax + b$.

Suppose the the quotient of $x^{100} - 5x^{88} + x - 4$ and $x^2 - 1$ is $q(x)$. Then

$$x^{100} - 5x^{88} + x - 4 = (x^2 - 1)q(x) + ax + b.$$

Because the relationship above holds for all x, it must hold for any particular x. If $x = 1$, then

$$(1^2 - 1)q(1) + a(1) + b = 1^{100} - 5(1)^{88} + 1 - 4 \quad \text{implies} \quad a + b = -7,$$

and, if $x = -1$, then

$$\left((-1)^2 - 1\right)q(-1) + a(-1) + b = (-1)^{100} - 5(-1)^{88} + (-1) - 4 \quad \text{implies} \quad -a + b = -9.$$

Solution 37. ───

Let us examine III. Pick the least positive value of an ideal $I \subseteq \mathbb{Z}$. Call it m. Every expression of the form km for k in $\mathbb{Z}$ must be in I, due to the definition of I. If there were a positive element n in I such that n is not a multiple of m, we could find a positive element smaller than m in I. Specifically, Euclid's algorithm tells us there exist integers a and b such that

$$am + bn = \gcd\{m, n\}.$$

This is a contradiction. Therefore, for each ideal I there is a positive m such that $I = m\mathbb{Z}$. Ergo, III is true.

Consider I. Euclid's algorithm tells us that there are a and b such that

$$am + an = d.$$

The number d is the smallest positive integer within $(m) + (n)$ because every linear combination of the two ideals, using coefficients in $\mathbb{Z}$, produces a sum which has the greatest common divisor of m and n as a factor. Since d is less than n and m and there is no positive number less than d within $(m) + (n)$, we know that I holds because the ideal must be of the form $d\mathbb{Z}$.

Lastly, we consider II. From the reasoning in the first paragraph, we know that $(m) = m\mathbb{Z}$ and $(n) = n\mathbb{Z}$. Therefore, it is clear $(m) \cdot (n) = mn\mathbb{Z} = (mn)$. Hence, II holds.

Options I, II, and III are true. We conclude that (E) is correct. ■

Solution 38. ───

Let us test some points. We know

$$\frac{dy}{dx}\bigg|_{(0,1)} = -\frac{0}{1} = 0.$$

Therefore, the slope field has a flat dash at $(0, 1)$. Indeed, the dashes should be flat for any point $(0, y)$, given $y \neq 0$. This eliminates (A). We also know

$$\frac{dy}{dx}\bigg|_{(1,1)} = -\frac{1}{1} = -1.$$

That narrows it down to (C) and (E). Notice that $|dy/dx|$ gets bigger as $|y| \to 0$, and $|dy/dx|$ gets smaller as $|y| \to \infty$, which eliminates (E). We conclude that (C) is correct. ■

Solution 39. ───

Since the unit-ball is always a distance of 1 from the origin, we can find the point on the plane closest to the origin. Then we will scale this point by one over its distance from the origin to find the point on the ball closest to the plane.

We need to find the minimum of $\sqrt{x^2 + y^2 + z^2}$ subject to the constraint $3x - 12y + 4z = 9$. The expression $\sqrt{x^2 + y^2 + z^2}$ is minimum if and only if $f(x, y, z) := x^2 + y^2 + z^2$ is minimum, so we will minimize the latter to reduce the complexity of calculations.

We will use the *method of Lagrange multipliers* on the optimization problem

$$\begin{aligned} \text{minimum} \quad & f(x, y, z) = x^2 + y^2 + z^2 \\ \text{subject to} \quad & 3x - 12y + 4z = 9. \end{aligned}$$

It says that

$$2x = 3\lambda, \quad 2y = -12\lambda, \quad \text{and} \quad 2z = 4\lambda$$

for some constant λ. Then a little algebra tells us

$$\left(\frac{27}{169}, -\frac{108}{169}, \frac{36}{169}\right) = \frac{9}{169}\,(3, -12, 4).$$

We can ignore the factor 9/169 because it will also scale the distance from the origin and then cancel when we multiply by one over the distance. So, we will simply multiply $(3, -12, 4)$ by the reciprocal of $\sqrt{3^2 + (-12)^2 + 4^2} = 13$. Hence, the point on the unit-ball closest to the origin is

$$\left(\frac{3}{13}, -\frac{12}{13}, \frac{4}{13}\right).$$

This is (D). ∎

Solution 40.

Let us consider option I. Suppose $A = [a_{ij}]$ and $B = [b_{ij}]$ for i and j in $\{1, 2, 3, \ldots, n\}$. Then the i-th row and j-th column of AB is

$$\sum_{k=1}^{n} a_{ik} b_{kj}.$$

If $B = A$ then $b_{kj} = a_{kj}$, and if $A = A^T$ then $a_{kj} = a_{jk}$. It follows that if $A = A^T$, then the entry on i-th row and column of A^2 is

$$\sum_{k=1}^{n} \left(a_{ik}\right)^2.$$

This implies

$$\mathrm{tr}(A^2) = \sum_{i=1}^{n}\sum_{k=1}^{n} \left(a_{ik}\right)^2.$$

Since $(a_{ik})^2$ is nonnegative for each i and k, the only way the trace can be negative is if $(a_{ik})^2 = 0$ or equivalently if $a_{ik} = 0$ for each i and k. Therefore, if $A = A^T$ and $\mathrm{tr}(A^2) = 0$, then $A = 0$. We have proven I.

Now we analyze option II. We will need to utilize some *determinant properties* to complete our analysis. If $AB = -BA$, then

$$\det(AB) = \det(-BA) \quad \text{implies} \quad \det(AB) = (-1)^n \det(BA).$$

Since

$$\det(AB) = \det(A)\det(B) = \det(B)\det(A) = \det(BA),$$

we know that $\det(AB) = \det(BA)$. Furthermore, $\det(AB)$ is non-zero because A and B are invertible. So,

$$\det(AB) = (-1)^n \det(BA) \quad \text{implies} \quad (-1)^n = 1.$$

This is only true when n is even. Option II is true.

Lastly, we turn our attention to option III. Consider

$$A = \begin{pmatrix} 0 & 1 \\ 0 & 0 \end{pmatrix} \quad \text{and} \quad B = \begin{pmatrix} 0 & 0 \\ 1 & 0 \end{pmatrix}.$$

Then A^2 and B^2 are both the 2×2 matrix with only zero entries. However,

$$A + B = \begin{pmatrix} 0 & 1 \\ 1 & 0 \end{pmatrix} \quad \text{implies} \quad \det(A + B) = -1.$$

Since $\det(A + B)$ is non-zero, $A + B$ must be invertible. Ergo, III is false.

We are ready to make our conclusion. Options I and II are true, and III is false. This corresponds to (C), so we select it. ∎

Solution 41.

We will use *Taylor's theorem* to approximate $f(1.5)$, but we need to make some observations first. Since our options are 0.5 units apart from each other, we cannot accept an error larger than that. We will use the Lagrange error bound to determine how many terms a Taylor series centered at 1 needs so that it is within half a unit of $f(1.5)$.

Let us find a few derivatives and evaluate at 1. We have $f(1) = 0$,

$$f'(x) = \frac{8}{x} \quad \text{implies} \quad f'(1) = 8, \quad \text{and} \quad f''(x) = -\frac{8}{x^2} \quad \text{implies} \quad f''(1) = -8.$$

We are ready to determine the necessary number of terms. The second derivative implies that the Lagrange error bound of a first degree Taylor approximation $T_1(1.5, 1)$ would be

$$\frac{\displaystyle\sup_{z \in (1, 1.5)} \left| -\frac{8}{z^2} \right|}{2!} (1.5 - 1)^2 = \frac{8}{2}(0.5)^2 = 1.$$

This is an unacceptable amount of error. Since $f'''(x) = 16/x^3$, the second degree Taylor approximation $T_2(1.5, 1)$ has a Lagrange error bound of

$$\frac{\displaystyle\sup_{z \in (1, 1.5)} \left| -\frac{16}{z^2} \right|}{3!} (1.5 - 1)^3 = \frac{16}{3!}(0.5)^3 = \frac{1}{3},$$

which is sufficiently accurate.

We will approximate $f(1.5)$ using the second degree Taylor polynomial of f. Since

$$T_2(x, 1) = 8(x - 1) - \frac{8}{2!}(x - 1)^2 = 8(x - 1) - 4(x - 1)^2,$$

it follows that

$$f(1.5) \approx T_2(1.5, 1) = 8(0.5) - 4(0.5)^2 = 3.$$

Pick (B)! ∎

Solution 42.

We would first like to remark on test-taking strategy. For most students, it would be wise to skip a problem like this because it is very time-consuming. Be mindful of the time constraint as you work through problems because it is a key consideration while taking the GRE.

We can use either the *method of Lagrange multipliers* or first semester Calculus to complete this problem. Let us use the former. The volume of our silo is $\pi r^2 h + 2\pi r^2/3$, which means

$$\pi r^2 h + \frac{2\pi r^3}{3} = 48\pi \quad \text{implies} \quad 3r^2 h + 2r^3 = 144.$$

The cost

$$C(r, h) := \frac{6}{\pi}\left(\pi r^2\right) + \frac{3}{\pi}\left(2\pi rh\right) + \frac{8}{\pi}\left(2\pi r^2\right) = 22r^2 + 6rh.$$

In summary, our optimization problem is

$$\text{minimum} \quad C(r, h) = 22r^2 + 6rh$$
$$\text{subject to} \quad 3r^2h + 2r^3 = 144.$$

The method of Lagrange multipliers tells us

$$44r + 6h = \lambda(6rh + 6r^2) \quad \text{and} \quad 6r = \lambda(3r^2).$$

Solving the second equation for λ, substituting into the first equation, and then solving for h yields $h = 16r/3$. So,

$$3r^2\left(\frac{16r}{3}\right) + 2r^3 = 144$$
$$\Rightarrow \qquad 16r^3 + 2r^3 = 144$$
$$\Rightarrow \qquad 18r^3 = 144$$
$$\Rightarrow \qquad r^3 = 8$$
$$\Rightarrow \qquad r = 2.$$

Since $r = 2$ is the only relative extreme, it follows that this must be the r which minimizes cost. The answer is (B). ∎

Solution 43.

We will first consider the general formula. If the first order partials of f exist and $\mathbf{r} : \mathbb{R} \to \mathbb{R}^2$ is differentiable in each coordinate, then

$$\frac{d}{dt}\Big(f(\mathbf{r}(t))\Big) = \nabla f\big(\mathbf{r}(t)\big) \cdot \mathbf{r}'(t).$$

Now we will consider our particular case. We have

$$\nabla f(x, y) = \langle \sin y, x \cos y \rangle.$$

Hence,

$$\frac{d}{dt}\Big(f(\mathbf{r}'(t))\Big)\bigg|_{t=0} = \langle \sin y, x \cos y \rangle\bigg|_{\mathbf{r}(0)} \cdot \mathbf{r}'(0) = \langle \sin 0, -1 \cos 0 \rangle \cdot \langle 1, 2 \rangle = \langle 0, -1 \rangle \cdot \langle 1, 2 \rangle = -2.$$

Fill in the bubble for (A)! ∎

Solution 44.

Let us take a look at a few iterations. Let S_k be the k-th iteration of the variable S. We have

$$S_1 = (\mathtt{h})^2\mathtt{h}, \quad S_2 = (\mathtt{h})^2\mathtt{h} + (2\mathtt{h})^2\mathtt{h}, \quad S_3 = (\mathtt{h})^2\mathtt{h} + (2\mathtt{h})^2\mathtt{h} + (3\mathtt{h})^2\mathtt{h},$$

etc. In general,

$$S_k = \sum_{i=1}^{k} f(x_i)\Delta x,$$

where

$$x_i = i \cdot \mathtt{h}, \quad f(x) = x^2, \quad \text{and} \quad \Delta x = \mathtt{h}.$$

The output printed S_n is the right Riemann sum of $f(x) = x^2$ over the interval $[0, 1]$. Since $n = 100000$ is large, the output is about the same as

$$\int_0^1 x^2 \, dx = \frac{x^3}{3}\Big|_0^1 = \frac{1}{3}.$$

This is (C). ∎

Solution 45.

Our task is to see if there is an observable pattern to the sequence A, A^2, A^3,..... We have

$$A^2 = \begin{pmatrix} 0 & 1 & 0 \\ 0 & 0 & 1 \\ 1 & 0 & 0 \end{pmatrix}$$

and

$$A^3 = A^2 A = \begin{pmatrix} 0 & 1 & 0 \\ 0 & 0 & 1 \\ 1 & 0 & 0 \end{pmatrix}\begin{pmatrix} 0 & 0 & 1 \\ 1 & 0 & 0 \\ 0 & 1 & 0 \end{pmatrix} = \begin{pmatrix} 1 & 0 & 0 \\ 0 & 1 & 0 \\ 0 & 0 & 1 \end{pmatrix}.$$

From here, it is not too tough to see that

$$A^{500} = A^{500 \pmod 3} = A^2 = \begin{pmatrix} 0 & 1 & 0 \\ 0 & 0 & 1 \\ 1 & 0 & 0 \end{pmatrix}.$$

Therefore, the correct answer must be (B). ∎

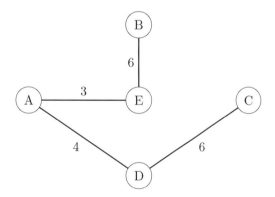

Solution 46.

We will use *Kruskal's algorithm* to determine a minimum spanning tree.

1. Pick edge AE because its weight is minimum.

2. Pick edge AD because its weight is minimum and no cycle is created.

3. Pick edge CD because its weight is minimum and no cycle is created. Do not pick DE because it would create a cycle.

101

conclude that the length of the thick band is

$$\frac{5\pi}{6} + 2\sqrt{3}.$$

Pick (E)! ∎

Solution 65.

We can use the *divergence theorem*. Let R be the interior of the cube with boundary S. Then

$$\oiint_S \mathbf{F} \cdot d\mathbf{S} = \iiint_R \operatorname{div}(\mathbf{F})\, dV = \iiint_R 0 + 1 + 1\, dV = 2 \iiint_R dV.$$

Since the volume of the unit cube is 1, we conclude that

$$\oiint_S \mathbf{F} \cdot d\mathbf{S} = 2(1) = 2.$$

This corresponds to (D), so select it. ∎

Solution 66.

All of the options are true. If

$$|f(x) - f(y)| \le |x - y|^2,$$

then f is a constant function. The proof is as follows:

$$|f(x) - f(y)| \le |x - y|^2 \quad \text{implies} \quad \left| \frac{f(x) - f(y)}{x - y} \right| \le |x - y|.$$

As we let y approach x, we see that

$$\frac{f(x) - f(y)}{x - y} \to f'(x) \quad \text{and} \quad x - y \to 0.$$

This implies $|f'(x)| \le 0$, which can only be true if $f'(x) = 0$. Hence, $f(x) = C$, were C is some constant. We conclude that (E) is correct. ∎

Glossary

Antiderivatives Useful antiderivatives.

- $\displaystyle\int u^n \, du = \frac{u^{n+1}}{n+1} + C, \quad n \neq -1$

- $\displaystyle\int e^u \, du = e^u + C$

- $\displaystyle\int \frac{du}{u} = \log |u| + C$

- $\displaystyle\int \sin u \, du = -\cos u + C$

- $\displaystyle\int \cos u \, du = \sin u + C$

- $\displaystyle\int \tan u \, du = -\log |\cos u| + C$

- $\displaystyle\int \frac{du}{1+u^2} = \operatorname{Arctan} u + C$

Arc length

- The arc length of the curve from $x = a$ to $x = b$ described by $y = f(x)$ is
$$\int_a^b \sqrt{1 + \left(\frac{dy}{dt}\right)^2} \, dx.$$

- The arc length of the curve from $t = a$ to $t = b$ described by $(x, y) = \big(f(t), g(t)\big)$ is
$$\int_a^b \sqrt{\left(\frac{dx}{dt}\right)^2 + \left(\frac{dy}{dt}\right)^2} \, dt.$$

- The arc length of the curve from $\theta = \alpha$ to $\theta = \beta$ described by the polar equation $r = f(\theta)$ is
$$\int_\alpha^\beta \sqrt{r^2 + \left(\frac{dr}{d\theta}\right)^2} \, d\theta.$$

Area with polar equations Consider the polar equation $r = f(\theta)$. The area between its graph and the pole from $\theta = \alpha$ to $\theta = \beta$ is
$$\frac{1}{2} \int_\alpha^\beta r^2 \, d\theta,$$
as long as there is no overlapping area.

Basis The set $\mathcal{B}$ is a basis of a vector space V over a field $\mathbb{F}$ if and only if the following hold.

- The set $\mathcal{B}$ is nonempty.

- Every element in V can be written as a linear combination of elements in $\mathcal{B}$.

- The elements of $\mathcal{B}$ are linearly independent.

Binomial distribution Suppose n independent trials are conducted, each of which can either end in success or failure. Let p be the probability success. Then the probability of exactly k trials ending in success is

$$\binom{n}{k} p^k (1-p)^{n-k}.$$

Furthermore, in a binomial distribution:

- The mean is $\mu = np$.

- The variance is $\sigma^2 = np(1-p)$.

- The standard deviation is $\sigma = \sqrt{np(1-p)}$.

Cardinal arithmetic Let A and B be sets.

- $|A| + |B| = |A \coprod B|$, where $A \coprod B$ denotes the disjoint union of A and B.

- $|A||B| = |A \times B|$.

- $\left| \{ f \mid f : A \to B \} \right| = |B|^{|A|}$.

- $|A| \cdot |B| = \sup\{|A|, |B|\}$ if $|A|$ or $|B|$ is an infinite cardinal.

Cauchy's group theorem Suppose G is a group and the prime p divides the order of G. Then there is a cyclic subgroup of G of order p.

Cauchy's residue theorem Suppose U is a simply connected open subset of $\mathbb{C}$ and f is a function holomorphic on $U \setminus \{a_1, a_2, \ldots, a_n\}$. Let C be a positively oriented simple closed curve whose graph is contained in U, and suppose $a_1, a_2, \ldots, a_n$ are inside of C. Then

$$\int_C f(z)\, dz = 2\pi i \sum_{k=1}^{n} \operatorname{Res}(f, a_k),$$

where for a_k a pole of order m

$$\operatorname{Res}(f, a_k) = \frac{1}{(m-1)!} \lim_{z \to c} \frac{d^{m-1}}{dz^{m-1}} \left((z - a_k)^m f(z) \right).$$

Characteristic polynomial The characteristic polynomial of an $n \times n$ matrix A is

$$p(\lambda) = \det\left(A - \lambda I \right).$$

The zeros of $p(\lambda)$ are the eigenvalues of A. If

$$p(\lambda) = a_0 + a_1 \lambda + \ldots + a_{n-1} \lambda^{n-1} + a_n \lambda^n,$$

the trace of A is $-a_{n-1}/a_n$ and $\det(A) = a_0$. If A has n linearly independent eigenvectors, then a_0 is the product of their eigenvalues.

Compact Consider the set X under some topology. A collection $\mathcal{U}$ of open sets is said to be an "open cover" of X if and only if

$$X \subseteq \bigcup_{U \in \mathcal{U}} U.$$

The set X is compact if and only if every open cover $\mathcal{U}$ has a finite subcover $\{U_1, U_2, \ldots, U_n\} \subseteq \mathcal{U}$ such that

$$X \subseteq U_1 \cup U_2 \cup \ldots \cup U_n.$$

Connectedness A topological space X is connected if there are no open, disjoint, and nonempty subsets A and B of X such that $A \cup B$ is equal to X. A subset U of X is connected if $U = A \cup B$ implies $\overline{A} \cap B \neq \varnothing$ and $A \cap \overline{B} \neq \varnothing$, whenever A and B are nonempty.

Derivative rules Suppose that f and g are differentiable on some domain D. Assume c and n are constants.

- Constant rule:
$$\frac{d}{dx}(c) = 0.$$

- Constant multiple rule:
$$(c \cdot f)'(x) = c \cdot f'(x).$$

- Power rule:
$$\frac{d}{dx}\left(x^n\right) = nx^{n-1}.$$

- Sum and difference rules:
$$(f \pm g)'(x) = f'(x) \pm g'(x).$$

- Product rule:
$$(f \cdot g)'(x) = f(x)g'(x) + f'(x)g(x).$$

- Quotient Rule:
$$\left(\frac{f}{g}\right)'(x) = \frac{f'(x)g(x) - f(x)g'(x)}{\left(g(x)\right)^2},$$

  where $g(x) \neq 0$.

- Chain rule:
$$(f \circ g)'(x) = f'\left(g(x)\right)g'(x).$$

Derivatives Useful derivatives.

- $\dfrac{d}{dx}u^n = nu^{n-1}u'$

- $\dfrac{d}{dx}e^u = u'e^u$

- $\dfrac{d}{dx}\log|u| = \dfrac{u'}{u}$

- $\dfrac{d}{dx}\sin u = u'\cos u$

- $\dfrac{d}{dx}\cos u = -u'\sin u$

- $\dfrac{d}{dx}\tan u = u'\sec^2 u$

- $\dfrac{d}{dx}\text{Arctan}\, u = \dfrac{u'}{1 + u^2}$

Derivatives have no "simple discontinuities" Suppose f is differentiable on the open interval (a, b) and c is in (a, b). Then

$$\lim_{x \to c^-} f'(x) = \lim_{x \to c^+} f'(x),$$

if both limits exist.

Determinant properties Suppose A and B are $n \times n$ matrices.

- The matrix A is invertible if and only if $\det(A) \neq 0$.
- If A^{-1} exists, $\det(A^{-1}) = 1/\det(A)$.
- For k in $\mathbb{R}$, $\det(kA) = k^n \det(A)$.
- The value of $\det(AB) = \det(A)\det(B)$.
- For k an integer, $\det(A^k) = \left(\det(A)\right)^k$.

Discriminant Consider a quadratic function $f(x) = ax^2 + bx + c$, where a, b, and c are real and $a \neq 0$. The discriminant is $\Delta := b^2 - 4ac$.

- If $\Delta > 0$, f has two real zeros.
- If $\Delta = 0$, f has one real zero of multiplicity two.
- If $\Delta < 0$, f has two complex zeros.

Disk method Consider the solid generated by rotating the region between $y = k$ and $y = f(x)$ about $y = k$. Then its volume from $x = a$ to $x = b$ is

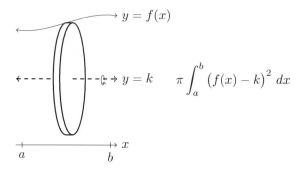

$$\pi \int_a^b \left(f(x) - k\right)^2 dx$$

The rotation about $x = h$ of the region between $x = h$ and $x = g(y)$ generates a three dimensional object. Its volume from $y = a$ to $y = b$ is

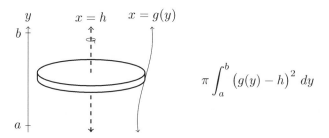

$$\pi \int_a^b \left(g(y) - h\right)^2 dy$$

Divergence theorem Suppose the closed surface S has outward orientation and is the boundary of a solid E, and $\mathbf{F}$ is a vector field with continuous first order partial derivatives. Then the flux of $\mathbf{F}$ through S is

$$\oiint_S \mathbf{F} \cdot d\mathbf{S} = \iiint_E \operatorname{div}(\mathbf{F}) \, dV,$$

where

$$\operatorname{div}(\mathbf{F}) := \left\langle \frac{\partial}{\partial x}, \frac{\partial}{\partial y}, \frac{\partial}{\partial z} \right\rangle \cdot \mathbf{F}.$$

118

e

$$e := \sum_{k=0}^{\infty} \frac{1}{k!} = \lim_{n \to \infty} \left(\frac{n+1}{n} \right)^n = 2.7182818\ldots.$$

Empirical rule The rule says that within a normal distribution about 68% of the data lies within one standard deviation of the mean, about 95% lies within two standard deviations, and about 99.7% lies within three standard deviations. So, if Z follows a standard normal distribution (i.e. Z follows a normal distribution with mean 0 and standard deviation 1), we have

$$P(|Z| < 1) \approx 0.68, \quad P(|Z| < 2) \approx 0.95, \quad \text{and} \quad P(|Z| < 3) \approx 0.997.$$

Euler's formula $e^{i\theta} = \cos\theta + i\sin\theta$ for all θ in $\mathbb{C}$.

Fermat's little theorem Suppose p is a prime number and a is an integer. Then

$$a^p \equiv a \pmod{p}.$$

If p does not divide a,

$$a^{p-1} \equiv 1 \pmod{p}.$$

First derivative test Suppose $f : \mathbb{R} \to \mathbb{R}$ is continuous on the open interval (a, b) and differentiable on $(a, b) \setminus \{c\}$, where $a < c < b$.

- If $f'(x) > 0$ for x in (a, c) and $f'(x) < 0$ for x in (c, b), then $f(c)$ is a relative maximum.
- If $f'(x) < 0$ for x in (a, c) and $f'(x) > 0$ for x in (c, b), then $f(c)$ is a relative minimum.

In other words, if f' switches from positive to negative at c then $f(c)$ is a relative maximum, and if f' switches from negative to positive at c then $f(c)$ is a relative minimum.

Fundamental counting principle Suppose there are n_1 ways for an event to occur, and n_2 ways for another independent event to occur. Then there are

$$n_1 \cdot n_2$$

ways for the two events to occur. More generally, if there are n_i ways for the i-th independent event to occur, where $i = 1, 2, \ldots, m$, there are

$$n_1 \cdot n_2 \cdot \ldots \cdot n_m$$

ways for the consecutive occurrence of the m events to occur.

Fundamental theorem of Calculus Suppose f is continuous on the closed interval $[a, b]$. Then

$$\int_a^b f(x) \, dx = F(b) - F(a),$$

where $F'(x) = f(x)$. Another version of this theorem, often called the "Second fundamental theorem of Calculus" states that

$$\frac{d}{dx} \left(\int_a^x f(t) \, dt \right) = f(x),$$

when f is continuous on an interval containing a and x.

Fundamental theorem of finitely generated abelian groups Let G be a finitely generated abelian group. It is isomorphic to an expression of the form

$$\mathbb{Z}^k \times \mathbb{Z}_{p_1^{\alpha_1}} \times \mathbb{Z}_{p_2^{\alpha_2}} \times \ldots \mathbb{Z}_{p_n^{\alpha_m}},$$

where $k, \alpha_1, \alpha_2, \ldots, \alpha_m$ are whole numbers and $p_1, p_2, \ldots, p_m$ are primes which are not necessarily distinct. Alternatively, G is isomorphic to an expression of the form

$$\mathbb{Z}^k \times \mathbb{Z}_{r_1} \times \mathbb{Z}_{r_2} \times \ldots \times \mathbb{Z}_{r_n},$$

where $k, r_1, r_2, \ldots, r_n$ are whole numbers and r_i divides r_{i+1} for all $i = 1, 2, \ldots, n-1$. The values of k and each r_i are uniquely determined by G.

Green's theorem Let C be a piecewise smooth simple closed curve in the xy-plane, which is oriented counterclockwise. Suppose D is the region bounded by C. Assume L and M are functions of x and y and have continuous partial derivatives on an open region containing D. Then

$$\oint_C L\,dx + M\,dy = \iint_D \frac{\partial M}{\partial x} - \frac{\partial L}{\partial y}\,dA.$$

Group The set G together with a binary operation $\cdot$ is a group if and only if the following properties of G and $\cdot$ hold:

- Closed: a and b in G implies $a \cdot b$ in G.

- Associative: for all a, b, and c in G, we have $(a \cdot b) \cdot c = a \cdot (b \cdot c)$.

- Contains the identity element: there is an element e such that $e \cdot a = a \cdot e = a$ for all a in G.

- Contains inverse elements: for all a in G there is a^{-1} such that $a \cdot a^{-1} = a^{-1} \cdot a = e$.

Heine-Borel theorem For all positive integers n, a set in $\mathbb{R}^n$ is closed and bounded if and only if it is compact.

Inclusion-exclusion principle For finite sets $U_1, U_2, \ldots, U_n$,

$$\left| \bigcup_{k=1}^n U_k \right| = \sum_{k=1}^n |U_k| - \sum_{1 \le k < \ell \le n} |U_k \cap U_\ell| + \sum_{1 \le k < \ell < m \le n} |U_k \cap U_\ell \cap U_m| - \ldots + (-1)^{n-1} |U_1 \cap U_2 \cap \cdots \cap U_n|.$$

Inflection point Suppose f is a twice differentiable real-valued function on the set $(a, b) \setminus \{c\}$, where $a < c < b$. A point $(c, f(c))$ is an inflection point of the graph of f if and only if $f''(x) < 0$ for x in (a, c) and $f''(x) > 0$ for x in (c, b), or $f''(x) > 0$ for x in (a, c) and $f''(x) < 0$ for x in (c, b). In other words, $(c, f(c))$ is an inflection point if and only if f'' switches signs at c.

Integral test Consider the continuous function f such that f is a positive and decreasing function. Say $a_n = f(n)$. Then either

$$\sum_{n=1}^\infty a_n \quad \text{and} \quad \int_1^\infty f(x)\,dx$$

both converge or diverge. Indeed, when the two are convergent, it can be shown the the remainder $R_N = \sum_{n=N}^\infty a_n$ of the N-th partial sum of the series is such that

$$\int_{N+1}^\infty f(x)\,dx \le R_N \le \int_N^\infty f(x)\,dx.$$

Integration by parts Suppose u and v are differentiable functions of x. Then

$$\int u\ dv = uv - \int v\ du.$$

Integration properties Suppose f and g are integrable real-valued functions over the closed interval $[a, b]$. Let α and β be in $\mathbb{R}$, and let c be in $[a, b]$. Then

- $\int_a^b \alpha f(x) + \beta g(x)\ dx = \alpha \int_a^b f(x)\ dx + \beta \int_a^b g(x)\ dx$

- $\int_a^b f(x)\ dx = -\int_b^a f(x)\ dx$

- $\int_a^b f(x)\ dx = \int_a^c f(x)\ dx + \int_c^b f(x)\ dx$

- $\int_c^c f(x)\ dx = 0$

- $\int_a^b f(x)\ dx \leq \int_a^b g(x)\ dx$, whenever $f(x) \leq g(x)$ for x in $[a, b]$

Intermediate value theorem Suppose f is a real-valued continuous function on the interval $[a, b]$. For each y between $f(a)$ and $f(b)$, there is a c in $[a, b]$ such that $f(c) = y$.

Inverse function theorem Suppose f is one-to-one and has a continuous derivative f' within some connected open neighborhood of $x = a$. Further, assume the graph of f within this neighborhood contains the point (a, b). Then

$$(f^{-1})'(b) = \frac{1}{f'(a)}.$$

Kruskal's algorithm The algorithm determines a minimum spanning tree for a connected discrete graph with weighted edges. Suppose the graph has v vertices. Begin by considering each of the vertices with no edges. Pick the edge of least weight unless it creates a cycle. Repeat the process until there are $v - 1$ edges.

L'Hôspital's rule Let f and g be functions differentiable on $(a, b) \setminus \{c\}$, and $g(x) \neq 0$ for all x in $(a, b) \setminus \{c\}$, where c is in (a, b). Assume

$$\lim_{x \to c} f(x) = \lim_{x \to c} g(x) = 0$$

or

$$\lim_{x \to c} f(x) = \lim_{x \to c} g(x) = \pm\infty.$$

Then

$$\lim_{x \to c} \frac{f(x)}{g(x)} = \lim_{x \to c} \frac{f'(x)}{g'(x)}.$$

Lagrange's theorem Suppose G is a finite group and H is a subgroup of G. The order of H divides the order of G.

Limit comparison test Consider the series

$$A = \sum_{n=1}^{\infty} a_n \quad \text{and} \quad B = \sum_{n=1}^{\infty} b_n$$

such that a_n and b_n are positive for all n. Suppose

$$\lim_{n \to \infty} \frac{a_n}{b_n} = L,$$

where L is possibly ∞.

- If $0 < L < \infty$, then either A and B both converge or diverge.

- If $L = 0$, then convergence of B implies convergence of A and divergence of A implies divergence of B.

- If $L = \infty$, then convergence of A implies convergence of B and divergence of B implies divergence of A.

Limits Some well known limits from Calculus.

- $\lim\limits_{x \to 0} \dfrac{\sin x}{x} = 1$

- $\lim\limits_{x \to 0} \dfrac{1 - \cos x}{x} = 0$

- $\lim\limits_{x \to \infty} \left(1 + \dfrac{1}{x}\right)^x = e$

- $\lim\limits_{x \to \infty} x^{1/x} = 1$

Logarithm properties The GRE assumes log is base e <u>not</u> base 10.

- $\displaystyle\int \frac{du}{u} = \log|u| + C$

- $\log x = y \iff e^y = x$

- $\log(e^x) = x$ and $e^{\log x} = x$

- $\log 1 = 0$

- $\log e = 1$

- $\log(xy) = \log x + \log y$

- $\log\left(\dfrac{x}{y}\right) = \log x - \log y$

- $\log x^y = y \log x$

Maclaurin series Suppose the n-th derivative of f exists and is continuous. The Maclaurin polynomial of degree n for f is

$$\sum_{k=0}^{n} \frac{f^{(k)}(0)}{k!} x^k.$$

If f is infinitely differentiable, then

$$f(x) = \sum_{k=0}^{\infty} \frac{f^{(k)}(0)}{k!} x^k.$$

Well known Maclaurin series include:

- $e^x = \displaystyle\sum_{k=0}^{\infty} \frac{x^k}{k!}$

- $\cos x = \displaystyle\sum_{k=0}^{\infty} \frac{(-1)^k x^{2k}}{(2k)!}$

- $\sin x = \displaystyle\sum_{k=0}^{\infty} \frac{(-1)^k x^{2k+1}}{(2k+1)!}$

- $\dfrac{1}{1-x} = \displaystyle\sum_{k=0}^{\infty} x^k$, where $-1 < x < 1$

Mean value theorem Suppose f is continuous on the closed interval $[a,b]$ and differentiable on the open interval (a,b). Then there is some c in (a,b) such that

$$f'(c) = \frac{f(b) - f(a)}{b - a}.$$

Method of Lagrange multipliers Suppose $f(x,y,z)$ and $g(x,y,z)$ have continuous first order partial derivatives, and there is a constant k such that $g(x,y,z) = k$. The relative extrema of f occur at points (x,y,z) that satisfy

$$f_x(x,y,x) = \lambda g_x(x,y,z), \quad f_y(x,y,z) = \lambda g_y(x,y,z), \quad \text{and} \quad f_z(x,y,z) = \lambda g_z(x,y,z)$$

for some λ in $\mathbb{R}$.

Necessary and sufficient condition for a function to be analytic The function $f(x+iy) = u(x,y) + iv(x,y)$ is analytic if and only if

$$\frac{\partial u}{\partial x} = \frac{\partial v}{\partial y} \quad \text{and} \quad \frac{\partial u}{\partial y} = -\frac{\partial v}{\partial x}.$$

Path connectedness A topological space X is path connected if and only if for all elements x_0 and x_1 of X, there is a continuous function $f : [0,1] \to X$ such that $f(0) = x_0$ and $f(1) = x_1$. If a topological space is path connected, then it is connected. However, the converse is false.

Power reduction identities Suppose θ is in $\mathbb{R}$. Then

$$\sin^2 \theta = \frac{1 - \cos 2\theta}{2}, \quad \cos^2 \theta = \frac{1 + \cos 2\theta}{2}, \quad \text{and} \quad \tan^2 \theta = \frac{1 - \cos 2\theta}{1 + \cos 2\theta}.$$

Probability properties Let X be the sample space, and A and B be events in X.

- $P(X) = 1$
- $P(\varnothing) = 0$
- $0 \le P(A) \le 1$
- $P(X \setminus A) = 1 - P(A)$
- $P(B) \le P(A)$ if $B \subseteq A$
- $P(A \setminus B) = P(A) - P(A \cap B)$
- $P(A \cup B) = P(A) + P(B) - P(A \cap B)$
- $P(A \cap B) = P(A) \cdot P(B)$ if A and B are independent events

Pythagorean identities Suppose θ is in $\mathbb{R}$. Then

$$\cos^2 \theta + \sin^2 \theta = 1, \quad 1 + \tan^2 \theta = \sec^2 \theta, \quad \text{and} \quad 1 + \cot^2 \theta = \csc^2 \theta.$$

Rank nullity theorem Suppose V is a finite dimensional vector space and let $T : V \to W$ be a linear map. Then

$$\text{nullity}(T) + \text{rank}(T) = \dim(V)$$

Ratio test Consider the series $S := \sum_{n=1}^{\infty} a_n$ and the limit $L := \lim_{n \to \infty} \left| \frac{a_{n+1}}{a_n} \right|$.

- If $L < 1$, then S converges absolutely.
- If $L > 1$, then S does not converge.
- If $L = 1$ or L does not exist, then the test fails.

Ring A set R is a ring if and only if it is an abelian (commutative) group under $+$ and the following properties of R and $\cdot$ hold

- Associativity: $(a \cdot b) \cdot c = a \cdot (b \cdot c)$ for all a, b, and c in R.
- Distributive on the right: $a \cdot (b + c) = a \cdot b + a \cdot c$ for all a, b, and c in R.
- Distributive on the left: $(b + c) \cdot a = b \cdot a + c \cdot a$ for all a, b, and c in R.

Second derivative test Suppose f is a twice-differentiable real-valued function such that $f'(c) = 0$.

- If $f''(c) > 0$, there is a relative minimum at $x = c$
- If $f''(c) < 0$, there is a relative maximum at $x = c$.
- If $f''(c) = 0$, then the test fails.

Second derivatives test Suppose that the function $f : \mathbb{R}^2 \to \mathbb{R}$ has continuous second order partial derivatives in some $E \subseteq \mathbb{R}^2$. Suppose the point (a, b) in E is a critical point, i.e. $f_x(a, b) = 0$ and $f_y(a, b) = 0$. Define

$$D := \begin{vmatrix} f_{xx}(a, b) & f_{xy}(a, b) \\ f_{yx}(a, b) & f_{yy}(a, b) \end{vmatrix} = f_{xx}(a, b)f_{yy}(a, b) - (f_{xy}(a, b))^2.$$

- If $f_{xx}(a, b) > 0$ and $D > 0$, then $f(a, b)$ is a relative minimum.
- If $f_{xx}(a, b) < 0$ and $D > 0$, then $f(a, b)$ is a relative maximum.
- If $D < 0$, then (a, b) is a saddle point.
- If $D = 0$, then the test gives no information.

Sine and cosine values in quadrant I To convert the radian measures in the first row to degrees, simply multiply $180°/\pi$.

θ	0	$\pi/6$	$\pi/4$	$\pi/3$	$\pi/2$
$\cos\theta$	1	$\sqrt{3}/2$	$\sqrt{2}/2$	$1/2$	0
$\sin\theta$	0	$1/2$	$\sqrt{2}/2$	$\sqrt{3}/2$	1

Slope and concavity of curves with parametric equations Suppose $x = f(t)$ and $y = g(t)$ are twice differentiable real-valued functions and t is a real number. At the point corresponding to t, the slope of the curve described by $\{(x(t), y(t)) \in \mathbb{R}^2 : t \text{ real}\}$ is

$$\frac{dy}{dx} = \frac{dy/dt}{dx/dt},$$

when $dx/dt \neq 0$. Furthermore, at the point corresponding to t, the concavity of the curve $\{(x(t), y(t)) \in \mathbb{R}^2 : t \text{ real}\}$ is

$$\frac{d^2y}{dx^2} = \frac{d^2y/dtdx}{dx/dt},$$

where $dx/dt \neq 0$.

Stars and bars A total of n objects are to be placed in k bins. The k bins are unique, but the n objects are indistinguishable. The number of ways to place the n objects in the k bins is

$$\binom{n+k-1}{n} = \binom{n+k-1}{k-1}.$$

Summation formulas

- $\displaystyle\sum_{k=1}^{n} a_k + b_k = \sum_{k=1}^{n} a_k + \sum_{k=1}^{n} b_k$

- $\displaystyle\sum_{k=1}^{n} c \cdot a_k = c \sum_{k=1}^{n} a_k$

- $\displaystyle\sum_{k=1}^{n} 1 = n$

- $\displaystyle\sum_{k=1}^{n} k = \frac{n(n+1)}{2}$

- $\displaystyle\sum_{k=1}^{n} k^2 = \frac{n(n+1)(2n+1)}{6}$

- $\displaystyle\sum_{k=1}^{n} k^3 = \frac{n^2(n+1)^2}{4}$

- $\displaystyle\sum_{k=1}^{n} a_k = \frac{n(a_1 + a_n)}{2}$, where $\sum a_k$ is an arithmetic series

- $\displaystyle\sum_{k=1}^{n} a_1 r^{k-1} = \frac{a_1(1 - r^n)}{1 - r}$, where $r \neq 1$

- $\displaystyle\sum_{k=1}^{\infty} a_1 r^{k-1} = \frac{a_1}{1 - r}$, where $|r| < 1$

Taylor's theorem Let f be a real-valued function defined on some set which contains the interval $[a, b]$. Suppose $f^{(n)}$ is continuous on $[a, b]$ and $f^{(n+1)}$ exists on the open interval (a, b), where n is a positive integer. Then for each x and c in $[a, b]$ there is a z between x and c such that

$$f(x) = \frac{f^{(n+1)}(z)}{(n+1)!}(x - c)^{n+1} + \sum_{k=0}^{n} \frac{f^{(k)}(c)}{k!}(x - c)^k.$$

Hence, f can be approximated by the polynomial

$$\sum_{k=0}^{n} \frac{f^{(k)}(c)}{k!}(x - c)^k,$$

and the error is less than or equal to the Lagrange error bound of

$$\frac{\sup_{z \in I} |f^{(n+1)}(z)|}{(n+1)!}|x - c|^{n+1},$$

where I is the open interval with endpoints x and c.

Trace The trace of a matrix A is defined to be the sum of the entries in the main diagonal of A. If tr denotes the trace function then $\operatorname{tr}(AB) = \operatorname{tr}(BA)$ for all square matrices A and B where the dimensions are equal.

Uniform continuity Consider the metric spaces (X, ρ) and (Y, σ). A function $f : X \to Y$ is uniformly continuous on $U \subseteq X$ if and only if for all $\varepsilon > 0$ there is a $\delta > 0$ such that

$$\sigma\left(f(x_1), f(x_2)\right) < \varepsilon \quad \text{whenever} \quad \rho(x_1, x_2) < \delta,$$

for all x_1 and x_2 in U.

Uniform convergence theorem Suppose $\{f_n\}_{n=1}^{\infty}$ is a sequence of continuous functions that converge point-wise to the function f. If $\{f_n\}_{n=1}^{\infty}$ converges uniformly to f on an interval U, then f is continuous on U.

Vector space A real vector space V is a set of elements such that the binary operations $+$ and $-$ are defined for elements in V, and for each real number c and element $\mathbf{v}$ of V, $c\mathbf{v}$ is an element of V. Furthermore, for all $\mathbf{u}$, $\mathbf{v}$, and $\mathbf{w}$ in V and for all c and d in $\mathbb{R}$ we must have

1. $\mathbf{u} + \mathbf{v} = \mathbf{v} + \mathbf{u}$

2. $(\mathbf{u} + \mathbf{v}) + \mathbf{w} = \mathbf{u} + (\mathbf{v} + \mathbf{w})$

3. There exists $\mathbf{0}$ in V such that $\mathbf{0} + \mathbf{v} = \mathbf{v} + \mathbf{0} = \mathbf{v}$

4. There exists $-\mathbf{v}$ in V such that $-\mathbf{v} + \mathbf{v} = \mathbf{v} + (-\mathbf{v}) = \mathbf{0}$

5. $0\mathbf{v} = \mathbf{0}$

6. $1\mathbf{v} = \mathbf{v}$

7. $(cd)\mathbf{v} = c(d\mathbf{v})$

8. $c(\mathbf{u} + \mathbf{v}) = c\mathbf{u} + c\mathbf{v}$

9. $(c + d)\mathbf{v} = c\mathbf{v} + d\mathbf{v}$

Volume of a parallelepiped The volume of the parallelepiped determined by the vectors $\mathbf{u}$, $\mathbf{v}$, and $\mathbf{w}$ is

$$\pm \det \begin{pmatrix} \mathbf{u} \\ \mathbf{v} \\ \mathbf{w} \end{pmatrix}$$

where the vectors are row vectors in $\mathbb{R}^3$ and the $\pm$ makes the determinate positive.

Washer method Consider the region bound between $y = f(x)$ and $y = g(x)$, where $f(x) \geq g(x)$ for x in the interval $[a, b]$. Then the volume of the solid from $x = a$ to $x = b$ generated by revolving the region about the x-axis is

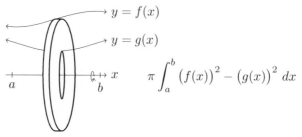

$$y = f(x)$$
$$y = g(x)$$
$$\pi \int_a^b \left(f(x)\right)^2 - \left(g(x)\right)^2 \, dx$$

Consider the region bound between $x = f(y)$ and $x = g(y)$, where $f(y) \geq g(y)$ for y in the interval $[a, b]$. Then the volume of the solid from $y = a$ to $y = b$ generated by revolving the region about the y-axis is

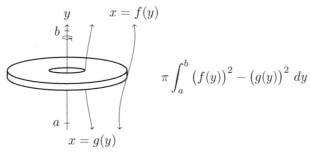

$$\pi \int_a^b \big(f(y)\big)^2 - \big(g(y)\big)^2 \, dy$$

Work Let $C := \{\gamma(t) : a \leq t \leq b\}$, where $\gamma : \mathbb{R} \to \mathbb{R}^n$ is differentiable in each coordinate. Then the work done by a vector field $\mathbf{F}$ over C is

$$W = \int_C \mathbf{F} \cdot d\gamma = \int_a^b \mathbf{F}\left(\gamma(t)\right) \cdot \gamma'(t) \, dt.$$

Made in the USA
Middletown, DE
24 January 2020